SAILING

A GUIDE

TO HANDLING

EQUIPPING,

MAINTAINING

AND BUYING

THE SMALL

SAILBOAT

by BILL WALLACE

A GOLDEN **HANDBOOK** GOLDEN PRESS | NEW YORK

PHOTO CREDITS:

Sam Chambliss: Pages 4, 7, 8, 10-11, 12, 15, 16, 19, 21, 22-23, 27, 30 right, 33, 35, 36 left, 37 right, 38-39, 41, 42-43, 45, 47, 51, 60, 75 top right, bottom left, 78-79, 80, 82-83, 90, 95 center, 97 top, 98 center, 99 center, 100 bottom, 103 center, bottom, 105 center, 111 right, 119 right, 122-123, 127, 128-129, 138, 140, 144-145, 151.

Morris Rosenfeld: Pages 24, 29, 32, 36-37 color, 40, 48, 52, 55, 56, 58-59, 62-63, 64-65, 68, 72-73, 74, 75 top left, bottom right, 76-77, 81, 85, 86-87, 88-89, 94, 96 top, 97 center, 98 bottom, 101 top, 102, 104, 105 top, bottom, 106 top, 107 center, bottom, 108-109, 111 left, 112, 114, 116, 117, 118, 120-121, 124-125, 126, 130-131, 136, 139 center, right, 148-149, 153, 160.

Bill Robinson: 99 bottom.

Contents

1

The Small Sailboat

■ Learning to sail, like learning to walk, is not so difficult. The skills come to almost everyone in time, but they do not come overnight. The best beginning is in a small, simple sailboat—one with a mast, a rudder, a mainsail, a foresail (called a jib), and not much more. It is with such a boat that our voyage by sail begins. This chapter is concerned with the nomenclature of sailboats, or the language of sailing. The nautical glossary may be foreign to the beginner, and perhaps ridiculous too. Not so. The terms are precise and must be understood by all, because sailing a boat is a combined effort on the part of the skipper, the sole authority, and his crew. When the skipper commands, his words must be understood and obeyed by all hands. To sail, one must first speak the language of sailing.

ANATOMY OF A SAILBOAT

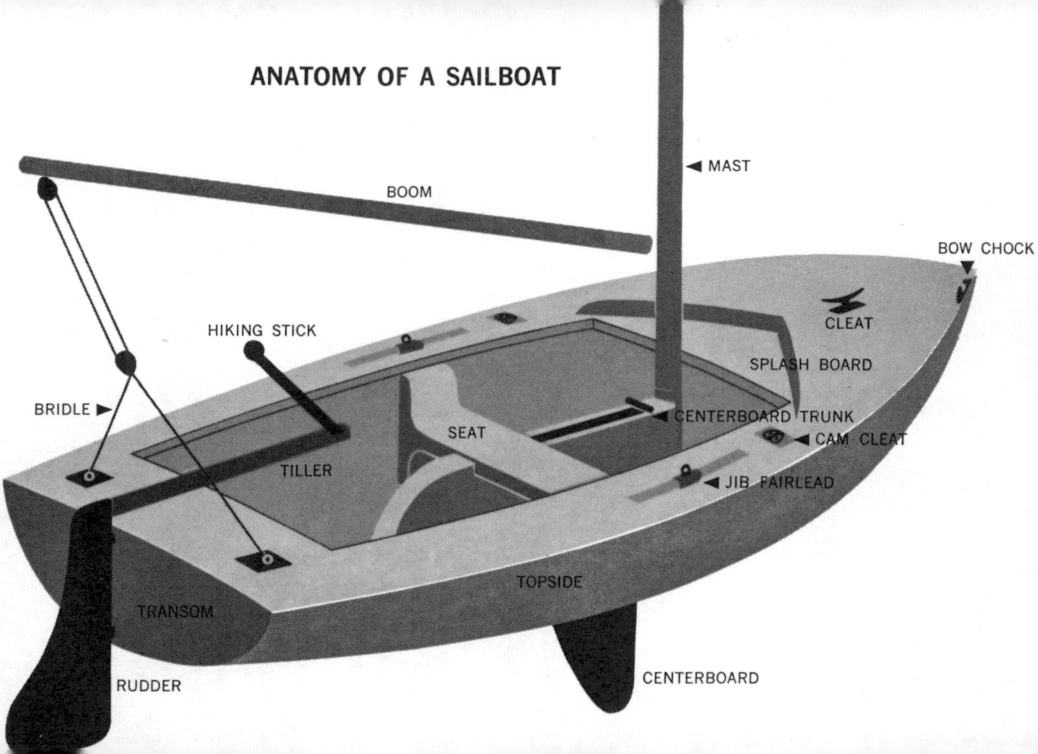

BOW CHOCK

CLEAT

SPLASH BOARD

CENTERBOARD TRUNK

CAM CLEAT

JIB FAIRLEAD

MAST

CENTERBOARD

TOPSIDE

SEAT

BOOM

HIKING STICK

TILLER

TRANSOM

RUDDER

BRIDLE

Stepping the mast means placing it securely in the sailboat

THE SMALL SAILBOAT

Most small sailboats are similar as to their equipment, and the pictures in this chapter are of a typical one: the Gannet. It is 14 feet long, has a fiberglass hull, and is sloop-rigged, meaning it has a mainsail and jib for working sails. It will float in only six inches of water. The forward part of the Gannet, or any other boat, is called the bow, the back end is the stern. When one goes toward the bow, one goes forward. When one moves toward the stern, one moves aft. Facing the bow, the left-hand side of the boat is the port, the right-hand side the starboard. The centerboard, which serves as a small boat's keel and helps prevent lateral drift, is raised or lowered through a slot in the bottom of the hull. In the Gannet the aluminum mast is removable. Erecting it in the boat is called stepping the mast. The diagram at left names other parts; their functions will be explained on succeeding pages.

7

Mainsail & Jib

■ The mainsail and jib are called working sails because they do the work of making the boat go. Almost all working sails today are made of Dacron synthetic cloth, which is very strong and hard to stretch. Dacron also resists mildew or rot, is difficult to stain or soil, and will last a long, long time.

The sail areas are identified in the opposing drawing. The battens—flat wooden or plastic ribs—are inserted into batten pockets and help a sail to keep its shape. The mainsail is secured snugly to the mast and boom at three points: head, tack, and clew. The head attaches to the main halyard, which the crew hauls to raise the sail up the mast. The tack bolts to a piece of hardware called a gooseneck fitting which attaches the boom to the mast. The clew secures to a fitting called the outhaul, which is pulled tight to the end of the boom. Halyard and outhaul provide the forces that stretch the sail at two extremities. Head, tack, and clew also apply to the smaller jib which snaps to the headstay. What's a headstay? Turn page.

Left: Gannet is ready for sails. Right: In go the battens

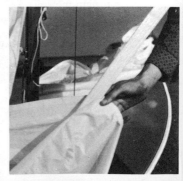

WORKING SAILS

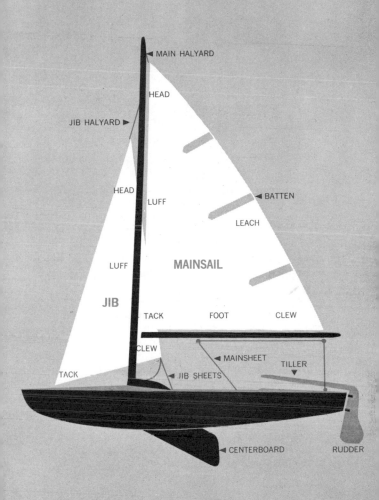

Left: Jibstay fitting. Right: Shroud is taped to spreader

Standing Rigging

■ The headstay, the backstay and the shrouds, which all support the mast, belong to the standing rigging. It "stands" permanently, as long as the mast is up. On a majority of sailboats this rigging is composed of wrapped wire strands that are extremely strong. The headstay runs from the bow of the hull to a point high up on the mast or, on some boats, to its very peak. In this case a boat is said to have a "masthead rig." The backstay runs from the top of the mast to the stern. This would be a permanent backstay, opposed to running backstays. Some boats have these: two stays running from a point high on the mast, but not the peak, to slides set aft on each side of the deck. They are movable, and, as will be seen, one usually is taut, the other slack. The stays running from the side of the boat to the mast are called shrouds. All stays attach to the

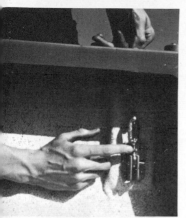
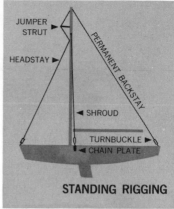

JUMPER STRUT

HEADSTAY ▶

PERMANENT BACKSTAY

◀ SHROUD

TURNBUCKLE ▶
◀ CHAIN PLATE

STANDING RIGGING

Shroud carries through the deck, securing to a turnbuckle

boat's hull by means of turnbuckles, adjustable thread-ed links with eyes that are rotated to tighten or slacken the stays. The turnbuckles secure the shrouds to metal chainplates built into the hull. Spreaders are small metal struts extending from both sides of the mast aloft. The shrouds lead over the ends of these struts and then to the mast at an angle, providing a stronger rig.

The larger the sailboat, the more support its mast must have. The standing rigging then multiplies. A second headstay is added, most often called a jibstay and securing farther down the mast. A second set of shrouds ends at the base of the spreaders. For additional sup-port, a second or even third set of spreaders may be added. Strength at the top of the mast may be pro-vided by a jumper strut, facing forward, with its accom-panying jumper stays.

11

Rigging the sheets for mainsail and jib is called reeving

Running Rigging

■ The running rigging of the small sailboat consists of
the ropes used to raise and control the sails. However,
rope in this sense is not a nautical word; instead we say
"lines." The running rigging consists of halyards, sheets
and guys, all movable and "running" about the boat.
Hence the name. The halyards, as we have seen, are
the lines used to hoist the sails. Starting from the cockpit, halyards run up the mast and through it by means
of sheaves. These are small wheels notched vertically
into the mast near the top. The halyards roll over the
wheels and then run back down to the deck. Each sail
has its own halyard and separate sheave. The main halyard hoists its burden up the after side of the mast
while the jib halyard lifts its sail up the headstay. The
pulling end of the halyard ties to a cleat located at the

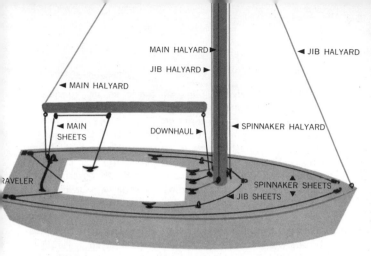

MAIN HALYARD ►

JIB HALYARD ►

◄ JIB HALYARD

◄ MAIN HALYARD

◄ MAIN
SHEETS

DOWNHAUL ►

◄ SPINNAKER HALYARD

RAVELER

SPINNAKER SHEETS

◄ JIB SHEETS ▼

Schematic drawing displays halyards in blue, sheets in red

forward end of the cockpit, but within easy reach.

The big point with halyards is to keep them clear. These lines, running aloft vertically, do intertwine and snarl until sails will not go up or down. Always untangle halyards aloft before raising sail.

Sheets are used to trim the sails — to alter their angle to the wind. The main sheet is always a single line running into the cockpit, but the common arrangement on the jib finds double sheets, one each for port and starboard sides. The main sheet controls the in-and-out movement of the boom and, therefore, the sail itself. The pull exerted by the mainsail is considerable, so the load on the main sheet is relieved by running it through a series of blocks (pulleys), located on the deck and on the underside of the boom. How does one bring in the 13 mainsail? Merely by pulling on the loose, or "running," end of the main sheet.

Jib sheets are not quite so easy. They secure to the jib at its clew and then run aft so that they can be handled from the forward area of the cockpit. Most often, the jib sheets are run aft inside the shrouds. When sailing, the jib will be trimmed to port or starboard, and the corresponding jib sheet will be the one holding in the sail. The other sheet, meanwhile, lies slack on the foredeck. However, when the boat changes course, the jib sheets change jobs. The one that was doing the work now lies slack and vice versa.

Sheets may be manila, cotton or Dacron rope. The latter two are easier on tender hands, but more expensive. Because it has stretching qualities, nylon will not do. Since sheets and halyards are the very lifeblood of every sailboat, the running rigging should be maintained in impeccable condition and rigorously inspected for wear. And until it becomes blindfold routine, the actual rigging of the sheets (called reeving) through the blocks should be done with care plus thought. On larger sailboats a combination of wire cable and rope is found for use first with main halyards, carrying their tremendous loads, then jib halyards, and finally jib sheets. The last few feet of these wire lines usually are spliced (woven) to a section of rope to make them easier for the sailor to handle.

Other elements of running rigging are guys, topping lifts and downhauls. The guy helps to control the spinnaker (see page 17). There are two kinds of topping lifts, one for the main boom (only on larger boats), one for the spinnaker pole. They hold up boom or pole.

Twisted halyards should be cleared before the sails go on

The lift on the spinnaker pole runs from the middle of
the pole to a block up on the mast, then to the deck. The
main topping lift merely takes the weight off the boom
when the mainsail is not set. The spinnaker downhaul
runs from the midsection of the pole through a block on
the deck and then to the cockpit. It lowers the pole and
completes the crew's control over the spinnaker. The
main downhaul, at the inboard end of the boom, pulls
down on the tack of the mainsail, thereby assuring the
desired tight fit along the luff of the sail.   **15**

Spinnaker pulling and crew bailing on an International 14

Fitting secures spinnaker pole to the mast in standard rig

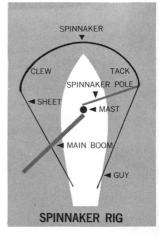

SPINNAKER

CLEW · TACK

SPINNAKER POLE

◄ SHEET · ◄ MAST

◄ MAIN BOOM

◄ GUY

SPINNAKER RIG

The Spinnaker

■ The spinnaker is a large, lightweight sail shaped like a cup, or a cone cut in half. It was first developed for racing, but now is found on many small sailboats to improve their speed and performance. It is used only for sailing downwind, when the jib loses its function of funnelling wind to the mainsail and flaps uselessly. At this point, the spinnaker's vast size and ability to face at right angles to the wind makes it a far more effective sail. Modern spinnaker cloth is lightweight nylon and comes in many bright colors that produce a striking effect when a week-end racing fleet sails its downwind leg. As with jib and mainsail, the spinnaker has its head, tack and clew, plus its own halyard. It is hoisted by the head to a point at or near the top of the mast. Because it is bulky, most sailors find it easier to control if it is raised out of a bag or a box. When up, the tack is secured to the outer end of the spinnaker pole. This attaches to the forward facing of the mast by means of a hook and eye or a socket fitting. The clew secures to a rope that leads outside the headstay and the shroud to the cockpit. The clew is trimmed—taken in or let out—from the cockpit. A similar rope, the guy, is extended from the cockpit to the outer end of the pole where the tack is secured. The big sail is controlled by combined trimming of sheet and guy. While the spinnaker is still in its box, the halyard, the sheet and the guy are all attached and rigged loosely. The sail is then hoisted, the tack secured to the pole, and the latter in turn secured to the mast fitting. A tug on both sheet and guy will break out the sail, enabling it to catch wind, like a parachute. Since the spinnaker is only used downwind, it is quickly dropped when the course shifts.

Fittings

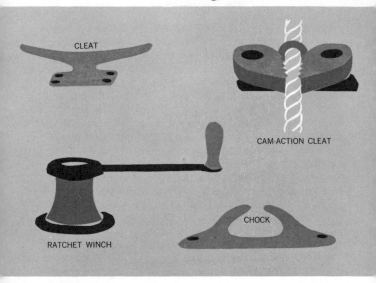

CLEAT

CAM-ACTION CLEAT

RATCHET WINCH

CHOCK

■ The many items of hardware aboard a sailboat are called fittings. They come in a variety of shapes, sizes and costs, and in materials that yachtsmen generally refer to as galvanized (inexpensive), bronze, plastic, or chrome (expensive). Starting at the bow, we find the headstay fitting and its turnbuckle which tightly secures the headstay. The painter (a short line which ties the boat to a pier) and/or the mooring line leads through the bow chock. On the foredeck lies a cleat for painter or mooring line. Near the mast, the jib sheets attach to the clew by means of a shackle which snaps shut.

FAIRLEAD

SHACKLE

Rudder fittings are called gudgeons and pintles

Around the mast at deck level a cluster of fittings is found. Halyard cleats are located here, either on deck or below it, in which case the halyard runs through the deck. Then there are cleats for the main downhaul, the spinnaker guy and topping lift. Also here is the gooseneck fitting that secures the boom to the mast. Another item, principally for racing craft, is the boom vang, a detachable fitting that runs from the underside of the boom to the deck. Its purpose is to hold the boom and mainsail down against actions of wind and wave when sailing before the wind.

FITTINGS

■ Fairleads are eyelet fittings secured to the deck. Sheets lead through the fairleads as they run aft into the cockpit, thereby enabling the crew to trim them easily. Fairleads or blocks on the mast also turn the direction of the halyards as they lead from the mast to their proper cleats at deck level. The jib sheets terminate aft at the cockpit by means of a cleat. But it is not always a good idea to secure the sheet by wrapping it around a cleat. The jib sheets need to be trimmed in and out very quickly, and to save time many sailboats are equipped with fast-action cam cleats or jam cleats. These lock in the sheet securely, but permit its quick release by the crew. For added purchase of sheets or halyards, a mechanical device called a winch is used. These have a revolving drum around which lines are given a turn or two. The larger winches have a crank handle which inserts at the top of the fitting. When the handle is turned, the drum revolves and in comes the sheet or halyard. On the after deck rests the traveler, a metal rod running across the stern to which is attached a block. One end of the main sheet leads to the block and ends there. The block slides back and forth across the traveler, permitting the mainsail to be trimmed to the proper angle when sailing to windward or off the wind. When on the wind, the main should be trimmed almost to the center of the traveler, but off the wind the block rides out to the end of the rod. On smaller boats, the traveler is replaced by a rope or cable arrangement called a bridle, which accomplishes the same mission. The rudder is secured to the transom by twin bolt-and-eye fittings. The insert bolts on the rudder are called pintles, while the two eyes on the transom are known as gudgeons. The rudder is fitted to the transom by inserting the pintles into the gudgeons.

Left: Pin secures tack of mainsail to the boom. Left center: Bolting tiller to rudder. Left below: Jib halyard leads through deck to cleat on mast. Main halyard is already cleated. Right center: Downhaul lowers boom in track on mast. Right below: Ball fits into slot on boom to secure boom vang

The Centerboard

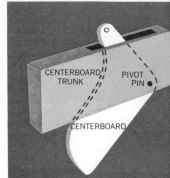

CENTERBOARD TRUNK

PIVOT PIN

CENTERBOARD

Centerboard on Gannet is controlled with block and tackle

■ A sailboat needs a centerboard or a keel extending beneath the hull for stability and forward progress. These underbodies resist the normal tendency of surface objects to float sideways with the wind or current. A sailboat with centerboard in the "up" position lets itself be pushed to leeward by the wind. (Leeward is the direction away from the wind source; windward is toward the wind.) With centerboard down, the boat can better hold a course to windward.

Centerboards are made of metal, wood, or plastic. They pivot on a pin and are housed in a trunk that fits over a slot in the bottom of the hull. They are pulled up or lowered by block and tackle. The daggerboard, found on small boats, is raised and lowered by hand. Centerboard-equipped craft can negotiate shallower waters than vessels with deep, immovable keels of iron or lead.

Trailering

Boat fits comfortably in trailer and mast goes on car top

■ Small sailboats, 20 feet and under in length, can take to the highways quite easily, thanks to modern trailers. Boat trailers serve many purposes. They give the boat owner an almost unlimited choice of places to sail. He also can drive his boat home, moor it in his own back yard, or store it on its trailer, thus saving the cost of yard bills. Stock trailers, priced from $125 to $300, are built to fit specific sailboats.

Boats are heavy objects to launch or to land, and trailers solve the problem. Many have frames that tilt, enabling the boat to slip directly into the water. Almost all have hand or power-operated winches that help a person to load the vessel by means of a cable attached to the bow. When launching or loading, the trailer is backed just past the water's edge, so that the boat will float when it slides off the trailer.

2

What Makes a Sailboat Go?

■ The wind—that is what makes a sailboat go. But the wind may sometimes work its muscle in odd ways; otherwise how can a boat sail into the wind, against the force which is pushing it? A not-so-odd way in which the wind powers the boat is by blowing upon the latter's exposed surfaces the sails—which transfer the resulting thrust to the hull. That is how the Egyptians, the original yachtsmen, navigated the Nile. They sailed up it, still do in fact, the prevailing northerly breeze pushing from behind and overcoming the opposing current. To go downstream against the wind, sails were dropped and the current did the work. Several thousand years later mankind had learned to sail at right angles (90 degrees) to the source of the wind and eventually into it at an angle of about 45 degrees. But not until the

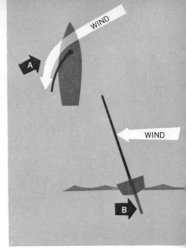

Mobjack sloop goes to windward

WHAT MAKES A SAILBOAT GO?

20th century and the advent of the airplane did man understand why a boat could sail into the source of the wind, at the 45° angle. An airplane wing is similar to a sail. Wind forces passing over the wing's surfaces create a lift on its topsides, a similar vacuum on the backsides of the sail. This vacuum tends to pull the boat ahead. Astounding! Many a time a novice sailor, upon learning of the leeward vacuum, takes his curiosity to the backside of the mainsail and feels for something, some movement, some power. Alas, disappointment. This lift or force cannot be seen or touched, but the laws of aerodynamics assure that it is there. Helping out is the underwater keel or centerboard which keeps the boat from being pushed sideways by the wind. This prevention also generates a force. And so there are two

26

Tremendous wind forces power a Naval Academy 44-foot yawl

forces, **A** acting on the sails, **B** on the keel or center-board. The result is similar to squeezing a watermelon seed between thumb and forefinger. The seed moves forward and so does the sailboat. In high-school physics this phenomenon is known as the parallelogram of forces, and in yachting, as sailing to windward. Although a boat will sail directly away from the wind's source, it cannot sail directly against this driving force. Therefore, it is obliged to follow a zigzag course, changing direction (tacking is the term) as the skipper knits his way to windward. The art of sailing is to control the boat so that it uses the wind in the manner desired by its occupants, whether this be moving to windward against the breeze or moving downwind with it. And that is what this chapter is all about—the art of sailing.   27

Sailing Into the Wind

■ A boat is capable of sailing into the wind, with the wind, or at right angles to it. These actions are called beating, running, and reaching, respectively. Sailing into the wind, or beating, at maximum efficiency and speed, requires the right combination of several factors: sail trim, helm, heel, crew position.

The jib, in combination with the mainsail, improves performance by channeling the flow of air across the main, thus creating a better pull-ahead vacuum. Why? Because the wind is funnelled through the slot between main and jib. However, the two sails must be trimmed in concert to present the best angles and surfaces to the wind. Sails that are trimmed into the boat too tightly present too little surface, almost a knife-edge, to the wind, thereby reducing the vacuum. The boat will respond sluggishly, tipping excessively if a good breeze is blowing. Sails let out too far break the airfoil effect and begin to flutter near their leading edges. This is luffing. It causes the boat to lose headway —in effect, to stall—and that's not good.

To obtain exactly correct sail trim is a delicate matter. The common way is to let out both main and jib until the luff appears, then bring them in until just after luffing has disappeared. Since wind and/or the boat's course are never constant, sail trim can require continual attention.

The helmsman has to steer the boat correctly and this too requires diligence. To go to the right, or starboard, the tiller (attached to the rudder) goes to the left, or port, and vice versa. A boat that is steered too closely into the eye of the wind—that is, inside the theoretical maximum of the 45° angle—will immediately

Jib and mainsail working together on a beat to windward

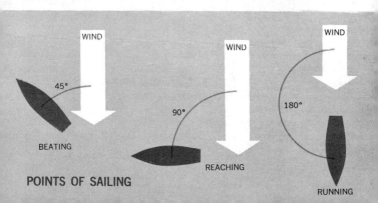

WIND

WIND

WIND

45°

90°

180°

BEATING

REACHING

RUNNING

POINTS OF SAILING

luff and its speed will decrease rapidly. Since a boat has no brakes, however, luffing can on occasion be a useful tactic. Sailing too close to the wind is called pinching, a fault, and if the boat could talk it would say ouch. The aim is to sail, to point, just barely short of inspiring a luff. Therefore, the helmsman should be looking, again and again, high up in his jib where the luff first appears. Conversely, a boat does not do well when it is steered too far off the wind with the sails sheeted in tight. But here there is no sign, such as a luff. There is, rather, a more subtle feeling of sluggishness, or, in a strong breeze, excessive tipping or heel. Yes, there is a great deal of **feel** in sailing and it cannot be gleaned from a book. The correct feel of a ship underway is memorable, however, and should be implanted early.

The common mistake of beginners is to allow the

Looking up slot between jib and main aboard a Highlander

boat to slide too far off the wind and then be unresponsive to the signals of inefficiency. The feel has not yet been properly felt.

The proper heel for most boats going to windward is for the rail on the leeward or down side to be 4 or 5 inches from the water. To have the rail underwater is inefficient. There are two remedies. The sails can be slacked off (inaccurately termed "spilling wind"), and/or the boat can be steered closer into the wind, thus creating a luff.

How the crew is seated can have much to do with the proper heel of the boat. Pounds of flesh on the high-side rail will counteract excessive heel. Every boat has its best position with regard to heel and weight distribution; when it is achieved a vessel is "sailing on her lines." How is this done? By experimentation, by feel.

Trio of Lightnings show proper heel in a light breeze

 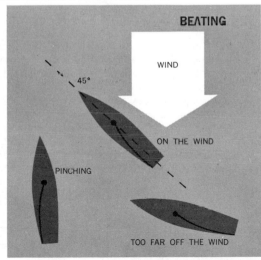

5.5-meter sloops racing downwind with spinnakers flying

Running

■ Sailing off the wind, before the wind, downwind, downhill, free, running—all these terms have the same meaning: the boat moves with, in the same direction as, the wind. For best results, the mainsail should be let way out, exposing much of its surface to the wind source. The spinnaker, designed for downwind sailing only, replaces the jib and is set forward of the headstay once the boat begins to go off the wind. When bellied out by the wind, the spinnaker will lift the bow of the boat imperceptibly, thus lessening the drag or resistance of the hull through the water. In theory, a sailboat running free should travel as fast as the air mass driving it, less the resistance of the water retarding the hull.

Boats without spinnakers, such as Stars, use their jibs downwind, although these are not awesomely effective and are difficult to control unless a rigid whisker-pole is used. This extends from the mast to the outside corner, or clew, of the jib and holds the sail in its most effective position, open-faced to the wind.

Running is usually easy sailing, except when the wind has strength. Then the helmsman must be cautious and steer a course more or less directly downwind, wary of the rolling seas behind, which can swing the stern around. If the breeze or the course should shift too drastically, so that the wind slips around to the front of the mainsail, a jibe will ensue. An accidental jibe, with sail, boom and sheets sweeping across the cockpit, can be dangerous to the crew and even capsize the boat. A beginner should practice sailing on a broad reach before running in a good breeze.

Whisker pole (arrow) extends the jib when running

Reaching

■ Reaching is the simplest of all points of sailing—and the fastest. To reach is to sail a course at an angle of about 90 degrees to the wind. We say "about" because there is nothing exact concerning a reach. In practice it can be all sailing courses between beating and running. A boat on a close reach sails a course less than 90 degrees to the wind, while on a beam reach it tracks a right angle to the breeze. A broad reach occurs at more than 90 degrees and comes very close to running. Sails are let out when reaching; the greater the angle away from the wind the more sheet being paid out. While on a broad reach, some boats can carry spinnakers and when they do, they are said to be sailing on a spinnaker reach.

While reaching, the parallelogram of forces is at its greatest and sailboats attain their best speeds. The record is 22.8 miles per hour, attained by a 17-foot Tigercat catamaran.

Provided a strong breeze does not overpower the boat, reaching is trouble-free and without the threat of jibing that complicates running. In fact, reaching is so simple as to become monotonous after a length of time. Reaching should be the first skill the novice attempts, together with trying for correct sail trim and a steady, straight course. For a practice exercise, try lining up the boat at right angles to the wind and choose a point on the horizon. Then steer for it. After a while this comes easy. At the same time, the right combination of sail adjustment should be sought. If the sails are trimmed too flat, or, conversely, slacked out too far, the boat slows down. By playing main and jib in and out, the skipper soon finds the trim that moves the boat fastest.

International 14 on broad reach with main slacked way off

Reaching provides thrill of speed

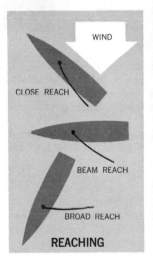

WIND

CLOSE REACH

BEAM REACH

BROAD REACH

REACHING

Tiller to leeward, jib free, Houn Dawg tacks

Tacking

■ To tack, or to come about, is to change the direction of the sailboat, to embark upon a new course. Tacking requires switching the sails' exposure to the wind from one side to the other, port tack to starboard, or starboard tack to port. (To differentiate these two, consider which side of the boat the wind is coming in from. If from starboard, the craft is on starboard tack. And vice versa.) When a boat tacks, the bow swings into the wind, through its point of origin, and then on over to the other tack. Of necessity, the pulling power on the sails stops when the boat is headed directly into the wind for a few seconds. So, the boat should be sailing at some speed before the tack is attempted to assure **36** enough momentum to swing the hull through the

Above: A crossing at close quarters

Left: Leader has tacked across foe

manouver. Otherwise, the sails will flap helplessly and the boat will wallow. How does one come about? The skipper issues a command of warning, "Ready about." Seconds later he commands, "Hard-a-lee," and swings the tiller so that the boat turns into the wind. The crew lets go the jib sheet, freeing the sail. It flutters as the boat is head-to-wind, then flops to the other side. The main boom and mainsail swing over, too, incidentally clobbering any upraised heads in the cockpit. When switching from one close-hauled tack to another, there is no particular reason to change the set of the mainsail; it should simply swing to the same position on the opposite side. The tack is over when the boat reaches its new course, and the crew sheets down the jib.

37

Jibing

■ Jibing is swinging the mainsail to the opposite side
while sailing downwind. In effect, it is a downwind tack.
The maneuver begins with the bow of the boat being
turned away from the wind, rather than into it. As the
wind catches the other side of the sail, the boom will
swing across the cockpit. The crossover, however, hap-
pens much faster in jibing than in tacking, as the sails
swing through a far wider arc. Unlike coming about,
when the craft loses momentum as it turns into the
wind, a jibing boat, turning away from the wind with
its sails filled, is likely to gather speed. And so let us
jibe. The skipper commands, "Ready to jibe," then
swings the tiller to windward, commanding again, "Jibe-

Jibing skipper swings boom over, but who has the tiller?

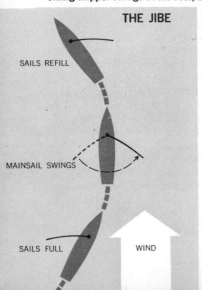

THE JIBE

SAILS REFILL

MAINSAIL SWINGS

SAILS FULL

WIND

oh." The bow falls off before the wind, the mainsheet is hauled in, first slowly, then as swiftly as possible, to control the crossover. If on a windy day the mainsail is not sheeted in, but left slack as the jibe begins, sail and boom will come crashing and sweeping across the cockpit like a scythe. Flying jibes like these are for competent yachtsmen only. During a jibe, the jib can be left to swing over by its own devices. The jibe ends when the skipper eases the tiller to midships, and the crew lets out the mainsail. It should go out fast in a breeze to prevent a knockdown (a perilous lean, close to capsizing). Jibes can go wrong, so they should be deliberate and controlled at all times.

Moment of the crossover aboard #580. Jib is on its own

Weather & Wind

■ "Red sky at night is the sailor's delight, while red sky in the morning is a sailor's sure warning." There is some truth to this old proverb, although more scientific ways exist to forecast general weather for sailing. The means are reading or listening to U.S. Weather Bureau forecasts, observing the barometer and familiar weather patterns in local areas, plus immediate reading of the weather signs provided by nature—for example, clouds in the sky. Because the sailboat's motor is the wind, impending weather is vital to the yachtsman.

In the northern hemisphere, weather moves from west to east. The weather maps in the newspapers show the high- and low-pressure areas across the country and these can be expected to move east at a speed of about 600 miles per day. Generally, the weather in a high-pressure area is clear and dry, with gentle winds. Low-pressure areas are likely to be stormy, with humidity, rain, and stronger winds. The day during which a low-pressure area is due to arrive will not be ideal for sailing. This will also be true on days when cold fronts (the convergence of hot and cold air masses) are scheduled to pass through. The locale, if not the exact time of the passing, can be determined from the maps. Cold fronts bring thunderstorms, often preceded by strong southwest winds. Winds within the storm are squally and tend to shift to northwest and northeast. In weak frontal thunderstorms, wind, rain, and lightning are not severe or long lasting, but the more severe line squalls contain danger in the form of knockdown winds. So know, from the forecasts, on what day the thunderstorm arrives and, from the cloud formations, at what hour.

Clouds with dirty bottoms like these often bring squalls

41

Some days bring pretty clouds, but no wind at all

WEATHER & WIND

The frontal thunderstorm can be anticipated by heavy vertical development of cumulo-nimbus clouds, which are dirty gray on the bottom and have anvil-shaped tops. Similarly, the localized air-mass thunderstorms, opposed to those brought by cold fronts, are indicated by rapid build-up of vertical cumulus clouds. Air-mass thunderstorms can be of short duration, although several may occur in the same area on the same day, with sunshine in between. Once a cold front passes through, moderate to fresh northwest to north winds can be expected for several subsequent days of fine sailing. Following the air-mass thunderstorms, weather is likely to return to what it was before the dark clouds came. Another hint of approaching thunderstorms is a dying breeze and a dead calm for a short period before the dark line of wind starts to move swiftly across the water. Signs of good weather are fleecy, broken, or isolated cloud formations high in the sky, with winds changing direction in a clockwise pattern, southwest to northwest, or east to south, for example.

Naval Academy yawls have all the wind they care to handle

The Beaufort Scale

This is a traditional scale used as a guide to estimate wind forces by actions of the waves. Woe to the sailboat caught at sea in a Force 7 gale or worse.

WIND FORCES	ACTION OF SAILBOAT	WATER CONDITIONS	WIND	WIND VELOCITY
1	STEERAGE WAY	RIPPLES	LIGHT AIR	1-3 KNOTS
2	SAILS FILL	SMALL WAVELETS	LIGHT BREEZE	4-6 KNOTS
3	SLIGHT HEEL	WAVELETS CREST	GENTLE BREEZE	7-10 KNOTS
4	GOOD HEEL	SMALL WAVES	MODERATE BREEZE	11-16 KNOTS
5	FIRST REEF	MODERATE WAVES	FRESH BREEZE	17-21 KNOTS
6	DOUBLE REEF	MANY WHITECAPS	STRONG BREEZE	22-27 KNOTS
7	HOVE TO	FOAM FLIES	MODERATE GALE	28-33 KNOTS

Force 8, Fresh gale, 34-40 Knots; Force 9, Strong gale, 41-47 Knots; Force 10, Whole gale, 48-55 Knots; Force 11, Storm, 56-66 Knots; Force 12, Hurricane, above 66 Knots.

3

Let's Go Sailing

■ To prepare the sailboat for action, called rigging the ship, is to follow a procedure which at first seems complex but later comes easy. First, let's dress the craft, or in nautical terms, bend on the sails. The order in which the boat is prepared may differ according to personal preferences. For example, should mainsail or jib go on first? If there is not enough crew to bend on both at once, the preference here is jib first, and in this manner. Initially, the tack should shackle to the fitting at the base of the jibstay (which may be also called the headstay). Along the leading edge of the jib (the luff) are a series of snap hooks (or hanks) and these snap to the stay. Then the shackle at the head of the jib is attached to the jib halyard, often by means of a through-bolt. If the jib takes battens, in they go and finally the sheets are

DEPARTURE	**LANDING**
Crew pushes bow from pier	**Make approach from downwind**

Crew trims jib before main	**Head into wind to slow boat**

Skipper trims main sheet	**Near dock crew goes forward**

secured to the clew of the sail. Some skippers like to raise the jib at this point to see if everything is in order, then lower it.

The two secured sides of the triangular mainsail, the luff and the foot, fit on the mast and boom, respectively, by means of slides which attach to a metal track. Many boats have a grooved slot in mast and boom which are made of aluminum or wood. With this type, the luff and foot of the mainsail are edged with rope which is fitted into this groove. Then the foot of the sail is extended along the boom, with the clew securing to the outhaul, and the tack to the gooseneck fitting by means of a pin or through-bolt. The slender battens are now placed neatly in their pockets and the main halyard is shackled to the head of the mainsail. The sails are now ready to hoist, mainsail first. The centerboard should be down, tiller and sheets freed. The mainsail goes up as high as it can, which may take muscle or a winch. Now the boat begins to come alive, like a dog on the threshold of the kennel. The boom crutch—usually an X-shaped support—is removed, the downhaul secured, and a quick check of the fit of the mainsail is made. Are all slides in the tracks, all battens in, all sheets and halyards clear? Next the jib goes up. It is needed before casting off the mooring because of the added control it gives to the boat when underway. To plan ahead—determine a course—before casting off, is to use brains. A sailboat needs time to get underway and become controllable, the less time the better for the skipper. A boat that departs a mooring on some kind of a reach will accelerate quickly and then can be maneuvered in any desired direction. So it is advisable to have the boat quickly fall away from the mooring and go onto a reach. First, the crew goes forward, un-

46

Clipping jib hanks to stay   Outhaul fittings on boom

cleats the mooring line and at the command, "Cast off," tosses the line and marker (a cork or a small floating buoy) away from the boat and its intended course. A real bad way to start a sail is to run over the mooring line and foul it in the centerboard or rudder. Meanwhile the skipper has put the tiller over to windward and the bow falls off before the wind, sails filling. If the wind is light, or there just is not room enough to fall off to a broad reach, a procedure called "backing the jib" may help. The crew grabs the jib at the clew, hauls it to windward across the centerline of the boat and holds the jib open to the source of the wind. The jib will quickly fill, driving the bow to leeward and at the same time generating speed. Backing the jib will also get a boat underway when it is "hanging in irons"—wallowing after losing momentum while coming about.

47

Right-of-Way Rules

■ "Here lies the body of Michael O'Day who died maintaining the right of way. He was right—dead right—as he sailed along, but he's just as dead as if he'd been wrong."—(Anon.)

It pays to be flexible on the waterways, especially in these days of the boating boom when a great many helmsmen, power and sail, have no notion of the Rules of the Road. The primary purpose of these rules is to avoid collision, but when the latter looms, the suggestion is to abandon the rules in favor of prudence, a word Michael O'Day did not recognize. The Rules of the Road are the regulations governing water traffic, and

Port tack boat, #203, has just enough room to stay clear

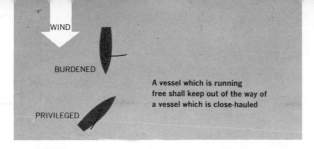

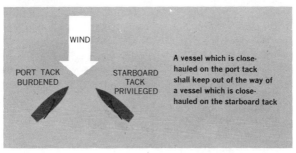

A vessel which is running free shall keep out of the way of a vessel which is close-hauled

A vessel which is close-hauled on the port tack shall keep out of the way of a vessel which is close-hauled on the starboard tack

Two fundamental rules of the road which prevent collision

they are the basis upon which maritime law is maintained. The rules cover all meetings, crossings, and convergings, and they establish which vessel is responsible for keeping clear of another. The Rules of the Road should be distinguished from the Yacht Racing Rules, which are something else again.

The Rules of the Road were written in the days when most ships were square-rigged and had a devil of a time sailing to windward. They maneuvered a good deal better when sailing off the wind, and so the rules make the downwind boats the "burdened" ones, requiring them to give way to those sailing to windward, or "privileged." By this rule, any vessel not working to windward—meaning one with sheets eased or pursuing a course other than to windward—is considered to be sailing free and, therefore, a burdened vessel. The general rule reads, "A vessel which has the wind aft shall keep out of the way of the other vessel." The additional basic Rules of the Road for sailboats are illustrated on these pages. In these compact drawings the vessels are entirely too close to one another. In practice, on the water, the burdened party should get out of the way a good deal sooner. In racing, however, it is permissible to shave things much closer, although not so close as to endanger either craft by running the risk of collision. This is plain bad sailing.

In relation to power boats, the rule says, "The power-driven vessel shall keep out of the way of the sailing vessel." But remember Michael O'Day. One of the universal gripes of sailing men is the lack of respect they seem to inspire in the minds of powerboat skippers who are, after all, the burdened parties. The wake of a powerboat going 12 knots or more can rock the wind right out of a small boat's sails on a light day, and it will take the craft some time to get going again. Alas, there is very little recourse for the yachtsman except profanity. In two instances the sailing craft is not the privileged one. Sailboats—all boats for that matter—must keep out of the way of any vessels fishing with nets, lines, or trawls, and in the rare circumstance when a sailboat overtakes a powerboat, the former must keep clear. In addition, common courtesy demands that the sailboat skipper refrain from pressing his privilege against ships warping in and out of docks or maneuvering in narrow channels, and against tugboats towing a string of barges. Common sense plus a sharp lookout by skipper and crew will eliminate most collisions.

Yawl is privileged but prudently luffs to let ship go by

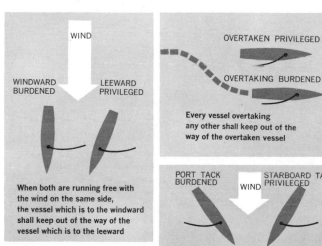

WIND

WINDWARD
BURDENED

LEEWARD
PRIVILEGED

When both are running free with
the wind on the same side,
the vessel which is to the windward
shall keep out of the way of the
vessel which is to the leeward

OVERTAKEN PRIVILEGED

OVERTAKING BURDENED

Every vessel overtaking
any other shall keep out of the
way of the overtaken vessel

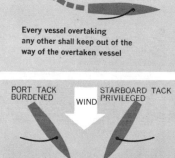

PORT TACK
BURDENED

WIND

STARBOARD TACK
PRIVILEGED

When both are running free, with
the wind on different sides, the vessel
which has the wind on the port side
shall keep out of the way of the other

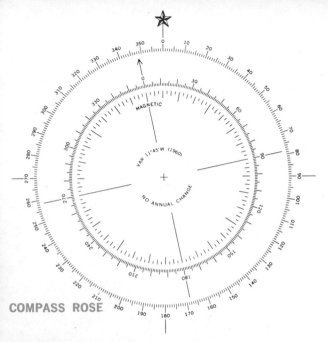

VAR 11°45'W (1960)

NO ANNUAL CHANGE

MAGNETIC

COMPASS ROSE

Radio direction finder takes bearings from radio beacons

Taking Bearings

■ A compass, a chart, and some amateur piloting will answer the classic nautical question, "Where am I?" Charts from the U.S. Coast & Geodetic Survey and the U.S. Lake Survey, sold locally, detail objects on land, on water, and underwater. Used with a compass, charts will pinpoint location by means of bearings, the straight-line direction of distant objects. The compass is related to the chart and vice versa by means of the "compass rose" found on the chart. A compass reading in degrees must first be converted into the magnetic reading, which means plus or minus the compensation of the compass error within the boat. This error, caused by shipboard magnetic attraction, is called deviation. It should be determined at the time of compass installation, with corrections listed on a deviation card. The magnetic reading in turn is converted to a true reading for chart purposes by use of the compass rose. The latter spec-

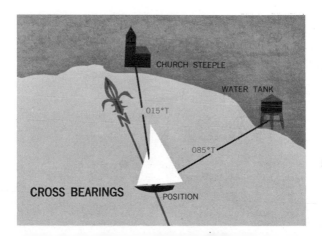

CHURCH STEEPLE

WATER TANK

015°T

085°T

CROSS BEARINGS POSITION

ifies the magnetic variation (difference in degrees between true north, measured to the North Pole, and the compass' magnetic north, measured to the magnetic pole in Canada).

Now let's determine a course. We start from Buoy 42 off Gull Point to go to Buoy 34 near Cedar Beach. A straight line is drawn on the chart between the two buoys. Using parallel rules, this line is then "walked over" to the compass rose and drawn through its center to the inner circle where magnetic degrees are shown. To the degree number located on this circle, add or subtract the deviation correction. The result is the course to be steered by compass to reach Buoy 34.

Next, let's take a "cross bearing." Sight over the compass at a distant object, say, a water tower on shore. Note the number of degrees that are on the sight line and, using the deviation card plus the chart rose, convert to a true bearing, 085 degrees. With the parallel rules draw a line on the chart through the tower at an

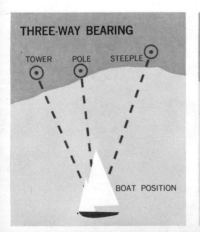

THREE-WAY BEARING

TOWER   POLE   STEEPLE

BOAT POSITION

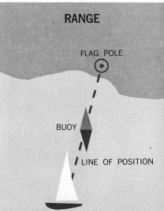

RANGE

FLAG POLE

BUOY

LINE OF POSITION

angle of 085 degrees true. This is a line of position, and our ship is located somewhere along the line. Where? Find another object on the horizon, perhaps a church steeple to the north. Take another reading over the compass, convert and draw the line on the chart, 015 degrees true. Where the two lines cross is the boat's position. Another method is the "three-way bearing." Take bearings of three objects and draw the angles through the objects on a piece of tracing paper. We now have three dots with lines drawn through each one. Move the paper over the chart until three dots line up on three objects. Extend the lines, and where they cross is the position of our boat. The easiest line of position to determine is the "range." When two objects, perhaps a buoy and a flagpole, line up one behind the other in the eyes of a distant observer, they are said to be "in range." On a chart, extend a line through the two; the observer's position is somewhere along the line. Find a second range and cross the lines to find position.

Hand-bearing compass is ideal for finding position at sea

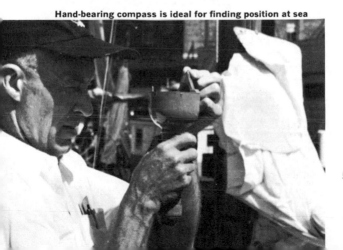

Tidal rip generates its own whitecaps on a windless day

Tide & Current

▪ Tide is the alternate rise and fall of ocean water governed by the gravitational pull of the moon and sun. Such waters are frequently spoken of as tidewaters to distinguish them from the inland seas or fresh-water lakes, which are not subject to this periodic variation of the water's surface. Current is the horizontal flow of the water. It is related to the vertical action of the tides, but also exists on non-tidal inland waters. Both tide and current, in turn, have a close relationship to the sailboat skipper. Depending on the kind of sailor he is, he can choose to fight them or to join them, but he can never ignore them.

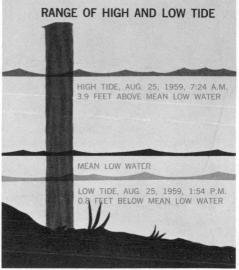

RANGE OF HIGH AND LOW TIDE

HIGH TIDE, AUG. 25, 1959, 7:24 A.M.
3.9 FEET ABOVE MEAN LOW WATER

MEAN LOW WATER

LOW TIDE, AUG. 25, 1959, 1:54 P.M.
0.8 FEET BELOW MEAN LOW WATER

The skipper who plans ahead can use the tidal flow to tremendous advantage. For example, if his craft is sailing along at three knots in the same direction as a three-knot current, his speed is doubled to six knots. But if the boat sails the other way at three knots, bucking a three-knot current, forward progress is absolutely nil. The idea, therefore, is always to know which way the current is moving and when; then plan the day's sailing to use this added push. Tide and current actions can be determined by observation or from publications. To check which way the water is going, one should observe the flow past a fixed object, such as a dock piling or a mooring can. The Government buoys are ideal. If the nun or can is leaning way over and the water is really gurgling by, the current is near its peak velocity. If the buoy is upright and there is no disturbance in the water around it, slack water is at hand and the tide is changing. It takes the experience of looking at many a leaning buoy to estimate current velocities with any accuracy. However, the tables published by the U.S. Coast and Geodetic Survey mark tide changes down to the minute, and current velocities to a tenth of one knot. The Tide Tables tell the time on each day of the year when the tide will reach high and low water at a host of

Oncoming yachts can check the current flow at this buoy

different locations. During a period of approximately 24 hours, 50 minutes, there will be two high tides and two low tides. On the charts, soundings are published in terms of mean low water, meaning the average depth of all low tides. The Tide Tables, in addition to giving the time of day of the highs and lows, also show the variations from mean low water. A high tide of 3.9 feet means the water will be 3.9 feet above mean low, while a low tide of —0.8 indicates the water level will go eight-tenths of a foot below the mean low-water mark. Current tables perform the same functions, giving the four times during each day when the current is either

Heavy lean of nun buoy shows run of stiff current

Page from Current Tables of Long Island Sound

Erect can, slight surface disturbance mean weak current

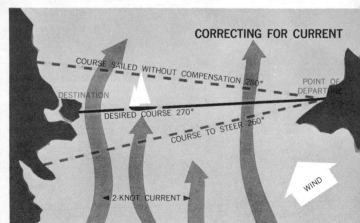

CORRECTING FOR CURRENT

COURSE SAILED WITHOUT COMPENSATION 280°

DESTINATION

POINT OF DEPARTURE

DESIRED COURSE 270°

COURSE TO STEER 260°

WIND

◄ 2-KNOT CURRENT ►

slack or at maximum flow and, at maximum, the velocity in knots. Although current is likely to be slack (not running) at nearly the same time as when the tide has attained a high or a low, the relationship between the two and their timing varies slightly from place to place, so separate books of tables are needed. Current is more difficult to measure than tidal height and may be affected more by temporary conditions, such as wind. So the Current Tables are not necessarily gospel. The best publications for the sailing man are the Tidal Current Charts—large, open books that show, with arrows, current actions for every hour of the day. Unfortunately, these charts are made up for only eight areas: Boston Harbor, Narragansett Bay, Long Island Sound, New York Harbor, Delaware Bay, Tampa Bay, San Francisco Bay, and Puget Sound, northern and southern parts.

A piloting problem arises when the boat sails neither directly with the current, nor against it, but rather takes it on the beam (at right angles), or the quarter (at a 45° angle). Suppose a boat is sailing east to west across a large body of water in which a two-knot current is running, south to north. The skipper will have to compensate for the tendency of the current to push him off course by steering farther to the south. In this event, the boat will "crab" along, much like an airplane in a crosswind, but ending up at the correct destination. Provided, of course, that the skipper estimates his compensation accurately. He should figure how long the trip will take him—say an hour—then conclude that within this hour the two-knot current will push him about two nautical miles to the north of his destination. Thus, he should chart a course that in theory takes him two miles south of his goal, and steer this course on the compass. The current will do the rest. **61**

Left: A spinnaker stop. Right: The sail's over

Sailboat Seamanship

■ Seamanship pertains to all skills used in operating a boat. It is the sum total of every sailor's knowledge, and how well he puts it to use determines how good a seaman he is. There is preparation behind every sail. The bilge of the boat must be emptied of water, by pump, or sponge and bucket. Sails and running rigging should be checked for wear, and prompt attention paid to the frayed rope, bent shackle, unscrewed turnbuckle, cleat working out of the deck, or loose snap-hook or slide on jib and main. If a spinnaker is to be used, it should be secured with thread (called stopping) for easier control when hoisting. Before leaving shore the sail is spread open on the ground. Then it is gathered together, but not folded, with the two leading edges, leech and luff, running side by side on top of the pile. Next the sail is secured with knots of breakable thread every 18 inches or so, and taken aboard. After the spinnaker has been run up the halyard, the wind's force will break the threads and open the sail. On a light day it can be opened by pulling on its sheet and pole.

Four hands can replace a jib snaphook better than two

Seamanship goes on public display at the completion of the sail, when the skipper aims to pick up a mooring in a crowded, populated harbor, or before a critical yacht-club audience. Moorings usually are small buoys floating on the water's surface which are connected by a length of chain to weights resting on the bottom. The problem is to maneuver the boat so that it will sail up to the buoy and then practically stop dead, so that a crew member can grasp the mooring, haul it aboard, and secure it to the cleat on the foredeck. Whenever possible, a mooring should be approached from behind (page 65) or from downwind, and preferably with the boat sailing on a beam reach to allow maximum maneuverability. When the mooring is close by, the boat should be turned into the wind, with sails luffing and speed reduced as the craft's momentum carries it up to the buoy. This is called shooting. The ability to gauge accurately the distance the boat will carry without help from the wind can only come with experience. A vague generality: in light, centerboard craft which quickly lose **63** headway, start to shoot two to three boat lengths to lee-ward of the mooring. Allow greater distance with heavier keel craft; they generate greater momentum. Overshoot-ing will make the crew's task of picking up the mooring almost impossible. Undershooting will halt the boat be-fore it reaches the mooring.

It is a good idea to lower the jib to reduce speed before the mooring approach begins. On a small boat—under 20 feet—the crewman, who is to fetch the moor-ing, will do best to lie prone on the foredeck, ready to grab. Aboard larger vessels, the technique is to kneel or stand on the foredeck and use a boat hook to spear the mooring line. Once the boat is secured, the mainsail should be dropped immediately.

Making a mooring in this harbor takes seamanship skill

To land at a dock also requires slowing down the boat to a virtual halt at a specific point. The penalty for poor judgment is greater because an overshooting boat can whack a dock and damage itself. Dock landings should be made in the same manner as moorings: approach on a reach, jib lowered, then shoot directly into the wind and up to the dock. When the wind blows into the dock, a downwind landing is required. Because it is difficult to check the boat's speed, this landing should be avoided by beginners. Their best bet is to drop all sails when 15 or 20 feet away from the dock, then float down to it with bare poles. The good seaman also plans an escape route—a way to sail out of trouble—should something go wrong with the landing.

Casting off from a dock with sails up and boat ready to go

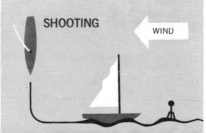

SHOOTING

WIND

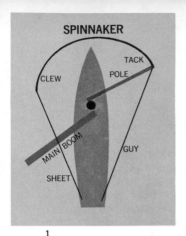

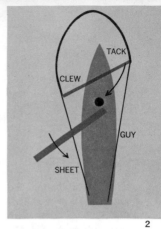

1

2

Jibing the Spinnaker

■ Jibing the spinnaker is the most difficult piece of sail handling of all. It requires good timing and co-operation between skipper and crew. As in the conventional jibe of mainsail and jib, the object is to alter the set of the sail in relation to the source of the wind. The boom of the mainsail shifts from one side to the other; likewise the spinnaker pole shifts from port to starboard, or vice versa. The aim is to keep the spinnaker full for a few seconds, preventing a collapse caused by the wind spilling out of the sail, while the pole is unsecured from the mast. There are several methods of jibing the spinnaker. The reverse-pole system is usually followed on small sailboats. Here are the steps. Compare them with the sequence of drawings above.

The guy is slacked, easing the pole which then will swing forward of its own accord toward the headstay. The pole is next removed from its fitting on the mast and the free end secured to the clew of the spinnaker.

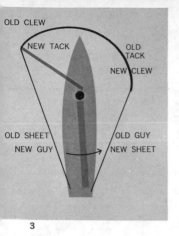

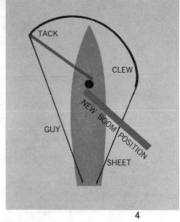

3

4

The two ends of the pole are now attached to the two corners of the sail. The mainsail is jibed over and the skipper sets the boat on its new course. Then the guy is cleared from the pole and attached to the sail at the tack. The end of the pole at the tack is now freed, brought back to the mast and secured to its fitting. The pole has been reversed, turned end to end. Although the sail and the running rigging remain virtually stationary, their names are reversed. The tack on the spinnaker becomes the clew, the sheet assumes the duties of the guy and vice versa. The new guy is secured to the pole at its outer end, the crew adjusts the trim of the spinnaker for the altered course, and the jibe is complete. The switching of the pole is done by a member of the crew standing on the foredeck of the boat. However, in many smaller sailboats, the spinnaker can be jibed from the forward part of the cockpit, provided the crew can reach the tack and clew. Long arms help. **67**

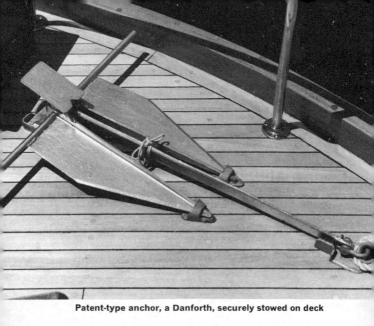

Patent-type anchor, a Danforth, securely stowed on deck

Anchors & Anchoring

■ Anchoring a boat to the bottom is much like hooking a screen door, although not quite so simple. The anchor itself is the hook and the problem is to set it in the bottom so that tide, waves or wind will not pull it out. There are several different kinds of anchors, but the three types that best suit sailboats are the yachtsman's, the mushroom, and the patent models. The yachtsman's anchor is a traditional type, heavy, clumsy to store on smaller boats, vulnerable to fouling its own anchor line. But when set firmly in the bottom it is as effective as any holding device can be. The simple mushroom has two uses: as a permanent holding anchor for a mooring, or, in a lightweight size, as a temporary grip. The larger mushroom takes time—days and sometimes weeks—to embed itself into a mud or sandy bottom, but once secured it can be stubborn about coming out. The small mushroom anchor of a size practical to keep on a sailboat, say a 12-pounder, will hold 500 or 600 pounds of boat on calm, protected waters free of current or strong winds. But for reliable holding against ravages of wind and sea, even a small sailboat deserves a patent anchor, such as a Danforth or Northill, which can be quickly dug into the bottom. A good solution for sailboats 16 feet long or more is to carry two: the small mushroom or "lunch" anchor plus the more muscular patent type. The important parts of the anchor are the stock, the shank, and the flukes. The Danforth's broad flukes really dig into the bottom and the manufacturer claims the harder the pull the deeper the anchor will work. An eight-pounder is recommended for sailboats up to 16 feet in length, a 13-pounder for those 16 to 20 feet, a 22-pounder for 20 to 40 feet over-all. For the small sailboat the Danforth offers the advantages of compactness and comparatively light weight, together with great holding power under a variety of conditions. The effectiveness of anchoring also depends upon just where one drops the hook. The best kinds of holding ground are sticky mud or clay, grass, sand or gravel. With the latter two, care must be taken to make sure the hook bites into the hard bottom. Soft mud and rocks make poor anchorages. The navigation charts show the nature of the bottom at likely anchorages. The novice yachtsman would do best to anchor where others have preceded him, however—and nowhere else.

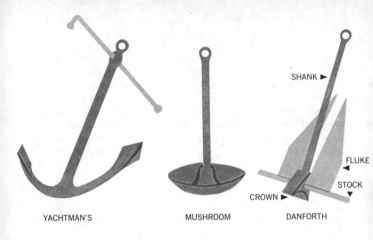

YACHTMAN'S   MUSHROOM   DANFORTH

SHANK ►

FLUKE ◄

STOCK ▼

CROWN ►

ANCHORS & ANCHORING

The line securing the anchor to the boat is called the rode. It can be of Manila rope, rope and chain combined, nylon, or nylon and chain. A short section of chain on the end will sink the line low to the bottom at a more effective hooking angle. Many skippers swear by nylon rodes because they are strong, will not rot, and stretch conveniently to cushion the shock when a boat takes a sharp tug at its anchor. For sailboats 20 feet and under, 100 feet of $\frac{3}{8}$-inch nylon is recommended. Add 25 feet more for boats 25 to 30 feet and make it a 150-foot line on 30 to 40 footers.

How much anchor line should be let out? The longer the better because length (called scope) increases holding power. For security against dragging the anchor in shallow areas, one should put out scope **70** equal to seven or eight times the depth of water beneath

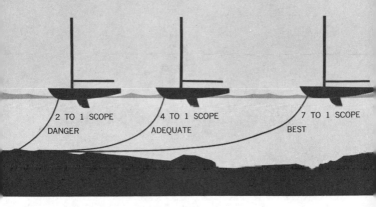

THE LONGEST ANCHOR LINE IS THE SAFEST

2 TO 1 SCOPE
DANGER

4 TO 1 SCOPE
ADEQUATE

7 TO 1 SCOPE
BEST

the hull. In deeper water less scope is required. A rule of thumb says a line twice the depth of the water has only one-fourth the holding power of a seven-times scope, and a line four times the depth will hold half as well as the seven-times scope. Whenever a sailboat drags its anchor, the immediate step is to let out more scope. But in crowded anchorages boats can easily collide unless all have the same scope and swing in the same arc as the wind shifts. This takes co-operation.

To drop an anchor one does not throw it out dramatically as though casting for bass. Wait until the boat has ceased to move forward, then gently lower the anchor over the side, paying out line until it goes slack, indicating the hook is on the bottom. The boat will next sag downwind some 10 to 15 feet and then the line is pulled taut, to dig in the flukes, and secured to a cleat.

4

When Sailing Gets Hard

Start of the 1958 Newport-Bermuda Race, a day when sailing was hard

■ When the wind blows in earnest, that is when sailing gets hard. Strong winds generate tremendous force and for the sailboat to combat them takes either countervailing brute strength or mechanical help. A 20-knot breeze on a mainsail will exert a lot of pull on the mainsheet. The sheet must be held down by a crew member or wrapped around a winch for a turn or two. Never secure it to a cleat, however. This is a sure way to invite a capsize. When a boat heels excessively, the sheet should be quickly let out, "spilling" wind so that the hull returns to its proper lines. Before a secured sheet can be uncleated, solid water may be pouring over the coaming into the cockpit. The inexperienced should stay ashore when sailing gets hard. For others, a stiff

Crew hikes to windward aboard an Atlantic on a mean day

WHEN SAILING GETS HARD

breeze can be fun—and safe, too—provided a few precautions are taken. If the wind is very strong and the
boat is being overpowered, the sail area should be reduced by reefing. To put in a reef, the mainsail must be
dropped and, if feasible, an anchor put out. The loose
sail is then furled neatly along the foot and secured by
reef points, which are short strings sewn into the canvas
at intervals. Reef points should be tied under the sail,
above the sail track; at tack and clew the sail is lashed
directly to the boom. Once the reef has been taken, the
shortened mainsail is raised again. Many small sailboats have roller reefing-gear, which is a godsend. Simply turning a crank rotates the boom and wraps the sail
like a paper towel on a roll. When the breeze pipes up,
it is also wise to secure all loose objects below, such as
dishes, coolers, anchors, instruments, and whisker or
spinnaker poles. All unnecessary gear in the cockpit—

cushions, cameras, binoculars—should also go below. On deck every movable object should be lashed down. Halyards must be cleared so that sails can be lowered immediately should conditions warrant. The crew is going to get wet, so it should don foul-weather gear and sit on the high side of the boat to counteract the heel of the hull. But not so far out as to inspire that chilling call, "Man overboard."

Mainsail secured, sloop is hove to, waiting out a gale

Left: Luffing main in squall. Right: Jib's off, mainsail next

Sailing at Night

■ Sailing at night involves most of the procedures used in the daytime, but the human responses are far different. There is many a skipper who prefers night to daylight sailing because of the silence, the solitude, and the self-sufficiency required.

Night sailing is all about lights: what ones to display for one's own safety and how to read the others. The smallest sailboats, such as dinghies or canoes, need no fixed light but should carry a flashlight to focus on the mainsail when other boats approach. Conventional sailboats up to 26 feet in length require a combination red-and-green light displayed at the bow and visible for at least one mile.

Clear, moonlit night can mean daytime visibility at sea

Such boats should also carry a flashlight to throw a white light on a sail when being overtaken. Sailboats from 26 to 65 feet must have separate sidelights, the green one on the starboard, the red to port. Actually, separate sidelights are preferred to the combination light on all sailboats, as they make it considerably easier for other vessels to comprehend the sailing craft's course and intent.

Auxiliary sailboats up to 26 feet under power must display a white light aft, showing all around the horizon, in addition to the combination red and green at the bow. Larger auxiliaries must also display a white light atop the mast.

77

Racing on a broad reach, these boats pass a lighted buoy

SAILING AT NIGHT

All sailboats should carry a powerful flash or searchlight for night work, such as picking up an unlighted mooring. Binoculars are even more effective at night than in daytime because they have light-gathering power far beyond the capacity of the human eye.

Our country's navigational system employs lights in three different colors—red, green, white—to mark obstructions or channels. When sailing into a harbor, green lights (marked G on the charts) are used on the port boundaries and red (R on charts) on the starboard ones. So, to keep clear, the skipper steers to maintain the green lights on his port side, the red ones on his starboard. Since it shows up better at night, white in combination with red or green is found on many lights. To further identify particular buoys or lighthouses, the lights may be fixed (continuous), flashing, or occulting (fixed but momentarily flashing out). If special caution must be observed, quick-flashing (one flash per second

Twilight racing in light air with bridge lights reflecting

or faster) lights are used. With all these available combinations, every light in a particular area will have its
very own signal which in turn is identified on the chart.
The night sailor can determine from the chart what
light he wants to find, then search in the appropriate
direction until he spots it. This is not always easy. Neon
store lights on shore, auto headlights, or street lights
shining through trees can cause confusion.

A sharp lookout should always be maintained at
night, particularly in crowded waters, for such things as
logs or unlit racing markers. It is easy to lose direction,
so the safest way to sail is from one checkpoint buoy
to another. Having all hands wear life jackets is also a
good idea. Decks are slippery at night, handholds in-
visible, and chances of falling overboard much greater.
If ordinary, common-sense precautions are taken, however, night sailing loses its dangers. And the pleasure
of a sail under the stars can be unforgettable.

Capsizing

■ Every good sailor has capsized at least once. In fact, no sailor's education is complete until he has experienced that hopeless, helpless moment when a sailboat discards the control of mankind and slowly lays itself down in the water. Landlubbers have fear of capsizing, but there really is nothing particularly dangerous about it, provided everyone aboard knows how to swim and sticks with the boat instead of striking out for shore on his own. Most sailboats that can turn over in the water have enough flotation (air tanks or a synthetic filler such as Styrofoam) to keep them from sinking. The place to be after the boat goes over, therefore, is in the water,

With main boom dragging water, this craft is going, going

hanging onto or sitting on the overturned hull. The party who swims away risks his life from cold water exposure, cramps, or fatigue. Sooner or later the overturned sailboat will be discovered and rescued, but until then the crew should conserve energy rather than thrash around in the water trying to save floating gear. A life is more precious than cushions, floor boards, or even a water-logged stop watch.

When it becomes evident the sailboat is going to capsize, the crew should climb to the high side. This is almost instinctive and, in any event, there won't be time to do much more. The idea is to stay away from

Although 110 is a keel boat, flotation tanks keep it up

Main halyard is slacked off, with rescue vessel alongside

CAPSIZING

the mainsail and avoid being smothered under it when
it hits the water. Prompt action by the crew can right
small centerboard boats after capsizing. (Boats with
heavy keels seldom tip over, but may swamp and require bailing.) The technique of righting requires, first,
lowering the centerboard, next slackening all sheets and
halyards, then hauling in the sails. If possible, lash sails,
spars, and loose objects to the boat so they will not float
away, and put out an anchor to windward to keep the
craft headed into the wind. The crew now stands on the
centerboard, with hands gripping the coaming, in hopes
that the combined weight will tip the boat back up
again. For added leverage, a line may be looped around
the shrouds and taken by one of the centerboard crew,
who then leans way back. The pull lifts the mast from

Standing on centerboard, skipper hopes to right his boat

the water and the hull rights itself. The cockpit will be full of water and must be emptied by bailing or pumping before the sail can go up and the voyage be resumed. Righting a sailboat takes much effort. It should be attempted only if the chances of success are good, if a rescue boat is standing by, or if the boat is in shallow water so the crew can stand. In fact, should a tow be available, it is always a good idea to take the capsized vessel into shallow water where it can be righted easily, safely, and at leisure. Powerboats operating around capsized sailboats should use caution and tow at the slowest possible speeds to prevent hull damage. There have been many cases of twin-engined powerboats backing their screws into sailboats and chewing the hull to sawdust.

Distress

■ A number of crises can arise aboard a boat. The common ones in the sailing fraternity, besides capsizing, are dismasting, blowing out sails, running aground, and losing someone overboard.

Masts break because one of the supporting stays of wire cable lets go and strains beyond the capacity of the stick are suddenly applied. Then there is the "compression" break that shatters the mast over an area of two or three feet because of tremendous pressures put to it. The modern metal masts can take a good deal more than wood. But even they will crumple on occasion. When the mast does come down, it should be cut away from the boat so that it does not bang alongside and poke a hole in the hull. The broken parts should then be lashed to the deck. Sometimes a mast can be put back together again on shore.

How does one get home when dismasted? The best way is to take a tow. Should none appear, put up a jury rig, using the boom or spinnaker pole as a mast to support some sail, perhaps half a jib or a part of the main.

Because of their great strength, modern Dacron sails seldom rip asunder as the old cotton-canvas ones used to do. Nylon spinnakers do go, and it is seldom practical to sew them together again. The danger with Dacron sails is tearing them on sharp objects after capsizing or a dismasting. Since working sails represent quite an investment, great care should be taken with them. Minor tears can be repaired by sewing. If a sail blows out while underway, there is nothing to do but take it off and put up the spare—if there is one.

Running aground is easy, getting off is hard. Centerboards give warning. When they hit something, they

This mast collapsed neatly just below the lower spreaders

Cause? A frayed mooring line. Ship now awaits high tide

This unlucky skipper waited too long before reducing sail

DISTRESS

bang and jump in the trunk. Often they can be raised and the boat sailed—or poled—to deeper water. A grounded keel boat is a far more serious matter. There are many ways to attempt freeing the vessel, but none is guaranteed. The easiest, in tidal waters, is to wait for high tide. The minute a boat grounds, the sails should be dropped so the vessel is not driven into an even worse position. It is safer to turn the boat around, or back it out, than to go on. In exceptional cases, sheeting sails tightly causes the hull to heel, and work clear.

Costly damage to keel was sad result of grounding

A boat may be poled off a shoal bottom, the crew pushing with the spinnaker pole. A powerboat might be able to pull the craft off. Then there is kedging, which means putting out an anchor and taking in the anchor line on a winch, ostensibly pulling the boat back to the anchor. Often, however, the anchor is merely pulled up to the grounded boat. To kedge successfully, an anchor must be well set in sand or rock. Mud is hopeless. The best way to get off a mud bottom is to rock the boat out. More advice? Read the chart and stay afloat.

Picking up the sailor who falls overboard calls for prompt, cool action. A preserver or ring buoy must always be within arm's length of the skipper so it can be thrown immediately. A member of the crew, not the skipper, should watch the man in the water and never, for a second, take his eyes off that person. In turning to pick him up, the boat should be swung through her normal radius so the course can be retraced. In most cases, a jibe is best. On final approach, head into the wind to slow the boat.

5

A Look at the Fleet

Far left: The yawl, Geor-jabelle, with spinnaker and staysail set. Left: The big 12-meter racing sloop Weatherly. Below: The schooner Nina under a full spread of canvas

■ One of yachting's great pleasures is merely to look at, and perhaps covet, the infinite variety of ships found at sea. "All boats are beautiful," is the claim of many a salt. The five basic types of sailing craft are sloop, cutter, yawl, ketch, schooner. The sloop has a single mast and so does the cutter, the difference being that the latter's is located further aft. The yawl has two masts, the smaller one (the mizzen) set aft, behind the tiller or wheel. On the ketch the mizzen lies forward of the tiller. The schooner has two or more masts, the mainmast being taller than (or as tall as) the foremast.

Hulls

Star boat has a V bottom with arc, hard chines, bulb keel

■ Sailboats come in three basic hull forms: flat bottom, V bottom, and round. All other hull types are variations of these. Each of the three has advantages and liabilities relative to the others, especially as concerns how and where the boat will be sailed. A heavy, round-bottom keel boat would make far less sense on a protected, inland lake than a lightweight, V-bottom, centerboard craft that can float in a foot of water.

Flat-bottom sailboats come mostly in small sizes, under 14 feet, where their virtues are displayed best. They are inexpensive and easy to build, they can sail in the shallow water of bays and rivers, and they go fast offwind in good breezes. As for faults, the flat-bottom hulls are poor performers in sailing to windward, they pound in a chop, and there is little room in them.

With either a keel or centerboard, the V-bottom hull is an ideal shape for the small sailboat. These are more seaworthy than flat-bottom boats, they go faster, have more room, and can be shallow or deep draft. There are many variations in these hulls—for example curved V's, arced V's—but all have the "chine" in common. This is the line where the boat's side and bottom meet, forming an edge. Sailboats are said to have hard or soft chines, the former in the case of a sharp corner, the latter when the corner is less severe or perhaps gently rounded. When a boat is heeled over, the leeward chine acts as a stabilizing second keel.

The round bottom can be very seaworthy, seldom pounding in a chop, but is most suitable in larger sizes. A small round-bottom sailboat would be expensive and very likely a wet boat as well, one that would soak the crew and roll from side to side when sailing before the wind. This type performs best with a heavy keel.

Planing hulls combine effectively the characteristics of V, flat, and round bottom. A planing hull tends to lift itself out of the water at high speed, thus reducing the drag in the water. The bottom is absolutely flat from midships aft. The forward sections are a compromise, what one might call a rounded V hull. When a planing hull is partially airborne, it displaces less than its total weight in the water, and very satisfactory speed results.

Although the shapes of boats are old, construction methods and surface coverings are very new. To a degree the new materials determine a boat's shape. For example, sheet plywood cannot be bent in more than one direction without great difficulty, so sheet-plywood boats are flat or V-bottomed. Fiberglass, on the other hand, always lends itself magnificently to curves and bends which add strength. Therefore, the round-bottom boat, which formerly was an expensive, hard-to-build hull when made of wood planking, is an ideal shape for fiberglass. Molded plywood also adapts well to curves, but it is more expensive to manufacture than fiberglass. Conventional wood planking has almost disappeared from small sailboat construction but is still found on large custom yachts with auxiliary motors.

Hulls with keels generally offer better performance, more stability, eliminate the risk of capsizing, but they are a liability in shallow waters and usually will cost more. Many cruising boats offer a compromise by having a centerboard which slides through a shallow keel.

92

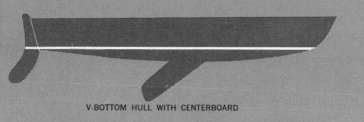

V-BOTTOM HULL WITH CENTERBOARD

ROUND-BOTTOM HULL WITH KEEL

PLANING HULL HAS FLAT BOTTOM

CENTERBOARD FITS THROUGH KEEL

Sailing Types

■ Most sailboats are designed for specific purposes. Each is likely to have characteristics that enable it to perform admirably in certain combinations of wind and water, and not so well in others. For example, the Alcort Sailfish below has no business ever wandering very far from shore. The point in these pages is to become familiar with different types of boats and to learn what they do best. (Prices are approximate and may change.) The four boats seen here have a wide variety of purpose. The Sailfish—essentially a sailing surfboard—is a wonderful toy for beach use, although in some areas it is raced seriously. The sloop, at right, is for day sailing or coastwise cruising. The catamaran, right, is a current vogue, perhaps because of its great speed. The Jolly, at top, right, is a planing hull with centerboard, fast and sensitive. The Sailfish comes in eight different models, wood or fiberglass, priced from $187 to $447.

SUPER SAILFISH MK. II: Mfr.: Alcort, Waterbury, Conn.

JOLLY: An 18-footer, it is one of many planing type English imports. It has molded plywood hull; is suited for cruising, racing. Similar to Flying Dutchman and 5-0-5. Price: $1,445. Mfr.: George O'Day Associates, 9 Newbury St., Boston 16, Massachusetts.

S-22: A 22-ft. sloop with fiberglass hull of keel-centerboard type, this has four berths and can be trailered by auto. It's often used as midget ocean racer on West Coast. Price, less sails, is $4,750. Mfr.: W. D. Schock Co., Newport Beach, Calif.

COUGAR: This catamaran is offered with plywood or fiberglass hull; price ranges from $1,800 to $2,100. Spacious boat, cat is 17 ft., 9 in. long; has 7-ft., 11-in. beam; weighs 320 lbs. Mfr.: Rebcats, 2727 29th St., N.W., Washington, D.C.

SAILING TYPES

X-TOUCHE: 48 ft. ocean-going sloop for cruising or racing accommodates eight. Broad-beamed hull has keel and centerboard. It's a proven winner, custom-built in West Germany in 1957. Designer: William Tripp, 10 Rockefeller Plaza, N.Y. 20.

VIKING 28: This heavy, 28-ft., imported sloop is for cruising only. Space is plentiful on board; hull is pine-planked. This costs $4,790; 23-ft. model is $3,590; both have auxiliary engines. Mfr.: Sailing U.S.A., 11 W. 42 St., New York 36.

INTERNATIONAL 500: This 31-footer comes with sloop or yawl rig at $14,700, less sails. It is suitable for modest distance racing, for overnight cruising; sleeps four. The 36-ft. model is $22,600. Mfr.: Cluett & Co. Box 398, Greenwich, Connecticut.

HARRIER: Was rigged as a cat boat as an experiment with handicap racing rules, but did not do very well. Normally a conventional Concordia 41-ft. keel sloop for cruising or ocean racing. Costs $32,000 new. Mfr.: Concordia Co., So. Dartmouth, Massachusetts.

MOTOR SAILER: A compromise between powerboat and sailboat. Sails, however, serve best as stabilizers. Custom-built 50-footer, it is loaded with comfort, cost someone dear. Well-known designer of motor sailers; Philip Rhodes, 11 Broadway, New York 4, N. Y.

TRITON: Introduced in 1958, this 28-ft. fiberglass yacht became an immediate success. With auxiliary engine, it is offered as a sloop ($9,590) or a yawl ($10,340). A fine cruising boat, it has berths for six. Mfr.: Pearson Corp., Bristol, Rhode Island.

97

SAILING TYPES

CORSAIRE: An inexpensive import, this 18-ft. sloop with plywood hull is for day sailing, limited cruising. Keel-centerboard type, it sleeps two. No auxiliary, but can take outboard. Costs $2,200. Importer: Nautica Corp., P. O. Box 26, Paramus, N. J.

BULL'S EYE: Long a favorite, this older design has been modernized by molded fiberglass hull. With small cuddy (shelter cabin), 18-ft. boat is fine for day sailing, junior racing. Cost: $1,845, less sails. Mfr.: Cape Cod Shipbuilding, Wareham, Massachusetts.

ELECTRA: This 22-ft. sloop with two berths can be either day sailer or overnighter. It is manufactured out of fiberglass. Prices start at $3,985. Cost does not include motor, but the hull is adaptable for inboard, or outboard. Mfr.: Pearson Corp., Bristol, Rhode Island.

DAY SAILER: Designed by Uffa Fox of England, this is 16-footer with big cockpit to accommodate six. Fiberglass hull means low maintenance. Priced at $1,495, without sails. Mfr.: George O'Day Associates, 9 Newbury St., Boston, Mass.

BUGEYE: This private yacht, a ketch, was custom-built for her owners following lines of historic Chesapeake Bugeye—a fast fishing boat with shallow draft and plenty of room. The lines of this Bugeye are considered as graceful as any. Designer: H. I. Chapelle, Wash., D. C.

AMPHIBETTE: This 24-footer has outboard power, a keel-centerboard hull, and can be easily hauled. Mast is stepped on cabin top, folds aft. For racing/cruising, berths for 4. Price is $5,500, less motor. Mfr.: Mt. Desert Yacht Yard, Mt. Desert, Me.

SAILING TYPES

SPRITE: Little 10-footer has convertible rig, so novice can sail with mainsail only, later add jib & spinnaker. Fiberglass hull; seats four youngsters. Price is $440, without sails. Mfr.: George O'Day Associates, 9 Newbury Street, Boston 16, Mass.

DOLPHIN: A 24-ft. auxiliary sloop with fiberglass, centerboard hull, this one is fine for cruising or modest distance racing. Options account for wide price range: $4,500 to $9,000 Mfr.: Geo. O'Day Associates, 9 Newbury St., Boston, Massachusetts.

GANNET: This 14-ft. centerboarder with fiberglass hull is simple to rig and to sail, ideal for beginners. A day sailer which can also be raced, it takes a crew of two or three. Price, new, $950. Mfr.: George O'Day Assoc., 9 Newbury St., Boston, Mass.

SKIM-AIR: A 9-ft. plywood dinghy with centerboard and single sail, this is craft for youngsters to sail. It holds two or three, depending on sizes, and will not sink. Cost is $235. Mfr.: Connecticut Boat Co., Steamboat Road, Greenwich, Connecticut.

KING'S CRUISER: An import that has wide acceptance in the U.S. Its 28-ft. wooden-planked hull with keel gives fine performance. It sleeps 4. Priced at $7,845 complete with sails. Importer: George Walton, Box 1528, Eastport, Annapolis, Maryland.

EL TORO: An 8-ft., cat-rigged, pram-type dinghy. Plywood hull weighs only 65 pounds, is inexpensive to build. El Toro is used for racing or as tender for larger vessels. Plans are available at $5 from Dan Herb, 3200 Deakin, Berkeley, California. 101

One-Design Classes

■ One-design classes are for racing, with day sailing or sheltered cruising secondary. To be one-design means that all boats of the class are built to the same set of plans and specifications, as nearly alike as man can make them, down to the last cleat and chock. Racing, therefore, becomes a true test of skippers and crew sailing comparable craft. Non-racing boats, even those with similar hulls, may have many variations in sails, fittings, or extra equipment which can alter performance. The one-design principle helps eliminate cost as a factor because one owner cannot spend more than another on similar boats.

On these pages are 16 of the leading types that have many racing fleets and their own class organizations, which set rules and conduct championship competitions. Write to the address given for information on the location of fleets and the names of builders.

INLAND LAKE SCOW: This is the very fast Class E 27-footer

REBEL: Among the first fiberglass sailboats, the 16-ft. Rebel is popular in the Midwest. Builder is Ray Greene & Co., Toledo 9, Ohio, which sells this centerboarder for $1,329. Information available at 3008 Ravenswood Boulevard, Toledo 14, Ohio.

NAT'L ONE DESIGN: A 17-ft. centerboarder, it has made shift from wooden, planked hulls to fiberglass. Despite limited sail area, the National O.D. is a lively boat. Its price, new, is around $1,250. Info.: 640 Sackett St., Cuyahoga Falls, Ohio.

HAMPTON: This sloop, 18 feet long, is a favorite in the area of Chesapeake Bay. With the centerboard up, she will float in about eight inches of water. Note how the twin spreaders support the tall mast. Information at: Box 43, McDaniel, Maryland.

ONE-DESIGN CLASSES

SUICIDE: This craft has an over-all length of 22 feet. Odd wishbone rig supports a loose-footed mainsail. Note how the mast has a rake aft. Suicides are found in several southern ports, principally in Florida. For information: Box 343, Palatka, Florida.

210: Sometimes called cigar box because of its hull shape, this 30-footer is of plywood construction, costs $2,900. A keel boat, the 210 draws 3 ft. 10 in., is raced in New England, Long Island Sound, and Hawaii. Information: 338 Jerusalem Rd., Cohasset, Mass.

LIGHTNING: A 19-footer, it comprises one of America's leading one-design classes. Over 8,000 of them have been built. This centerboard boat costs about $1,900 when new. Fleets are found from coast to coast. Info.: 308 Center St., South Haven, Mich.

SNIPE: The largest and among the oldest racing classes, it numbers over 11,000 boats built in 30 years. The hull is 15½ feet long, and fiberglass construction has recently been introduced. New boats cost $1,100 up. Info.: 655 Weber Av., Akron 3, Ohio.

INTERNAT'L 14: Famous racing class in U.S., Canada, and Britain. The 14-ft. hulls are molded plywood or fiberglass. A centerboarder, the 14 is a planing type, swift and sensitive. Price: $1,375. Info.: Dr. S. H. Walker, Luce Creek Dr., Annapolis, Md.

BLUE JAY: A versatile 13½-ft. sloop that enjoys great popularity as junior trainer with several hundred sold each year. Prices start at $685. Hull is sheet plywood with a centerboard. Info.: Robert Sparkman, 11 East 44th St., New York 17, N.Y. **105**

ONE-DESIGN CLASSES

THISTLE: This molded plywood 17-footer can be raced extensively and also take the family sailing. The overlapping jib adds to performance. New boats cost about $1,800, are available in fiberglass. Info.: Apt. 1439, 2025 Peachtree, N.E., Atlanta, Ga.

5-0-5: Built with a planing hull, it is 16½-ft. long, and British in origin. Construction is molded plywood. Extremely fast, these centerboarders provide tremendous thrills, but they're not designed for beginners. Info.: 9 Newbury St., Boston, Mass.

LIDO 14: This 14-ft. fiberglass sloop has its aluminum mast stepped at the deck and hinged so it will fold down for trailering. Rig features loose-footed main, overlapping jib. Price: $975. Info.: 504 29th St., Newport Beach, Calif.

STAR: The oldest one-design class, with fleets located in many parts of the world. This is a keel boat with a planked hull, 23 feet long. Strictly for racing with a crew of two. Info.: International Star Class, 51 East 42nd St., N. Y. 17.

110: A smaller sister ship of the 210, this 24-ft. boat has plywood hull with bulb keel. The large overlapping head-sail is called a genoa jib, a type found on many racing boats. New, a 110 costs $1,-595. Information at: 505 So. Birney, Bay City, Michigan.

RAVEN: A lively 24-footer, this craft has planing hull of molded plywood or fiber-glass; a centerboard. Ample sail area keeps crew busy in breeze. New boat is $2,945. Popular in Northeast, Mid-west. Information: Bay View Yacht Club, Detroit, Mich. **107**

6
Racing

■ Because it is a natural inclination to see if I can sail my boat faster than the other fellow can sail his, racing quickly becomes a goal for many beginning yachtsmen. Learning to race sharpens one's skills, teaches a great deal in a very short time, and makes better seamen of the participants for every kind of situation they may face on the water. Racing demands that a boat be sailed at peak efficiency, with sails in proper trim at all times. Even when just loafing or cruising, the racing yachtsman cannot abide sailing aboard a sloppy vessel, indifferently trimmed. His are good habits. Yacht racing, at its highest level, is complex, competitive, and exciting. And although it is more than 120 years old, its adherents continue to widen the frontiers of their knowledge with new techniques and new materials.

Crew aids skipper in spotting marks and the competition

The Crew

■ Racing requires a high order of teamwork between skipper and crew. The ideal crewman has been described as "strong as a gorilla, light as a cat, and with every tooth a marlinespike." There are few enough who meet these specifications; most skippers will settle for competitive spirit, willingness to learn, and some agility. A good crewman acts without being told, knows his duties and the habits of his skipper, and serves as another pair of eyes at spotting marks and the opposition. At the start of a race, the skipper has so much on his mind he may entrust the second-by-second timing between signals and the operation of the stop watch to a member of the crew. Although yacht races can be heated affairs, and an occasional burst of temper is not unknown, the sport does have its successful husband-and-

110

Crew's weight helps, way forward (left) or hiking (right)

wife racing teams. However, the record shows that the husband almost always serves as the skipper.

Occasionally, a newcomer to yacht racing will ask if there is a disposition to disregard or flaunt the rules. The answer is no. The spirit in the sport is one of fair play, for all yachtsmen recognize that to honor the rules is to permit competition, to dishonor them is to invite chaos. Specifically, racing yachtsmen try to avoid collision at all times. Oh, they certainly debate who was where when and who did what to whom in the hearings of protests. One competitor should always protest against another when an infraction of the rules is alleged. However, everyone respects Rule 31, which says, "A yacht shall attempt to win a race only by fair sailing and superior speed and skill."

The Start

■ The start often is the most important part of the race. Seconds and distance lost here are difficult to regain. The starting line is set by the race committee and it extends from the anchored committee boat to a buoy or mark several dozen yards away. The perfect line is set perpendicular to the direction of the wind, with the boats required to sail to windward on the opening leg of the course. There are, however, imperfectly set lines and, on occasion, downwind starts to leeward. The committee indicates the course by means of signals, either code flags or letters and numbers. Each contestant has a race circular listing the signals which tell where the boats are supposed to go during the race. The race

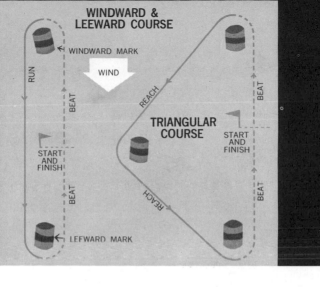

WINDWARD &
LEEWARD COURSE

WINDWARD MARK

RUN

BEAT

WIND

REACH

TRIANGULAR
COURSE

BEAT

START AND FINISH

BEAT

START AND FINISH

BEAT

REACH

BEAT

LEEWARD MARK

committee fires a warning shot with a signal cannon or pistol ten minutes before the race is to start, a preparatory shot at five minutes, and then the starting gun. The object? To cross the starting line exactly as the gun fires with the boat moving at its best speed. Any part of a sailboat which is on or over the line before the start will result in a recall for that vessel. It must go back across the line, staying out of the way of all the others, turn about, and start properly. To know exactly the minutes and seconds before the start, someone in the crew should carry a stop watch and shout the time remaining to the skipper. A proper start requires planning. One should figure out where on the line to start, taking into 113 account the location of the turning mark at the end of the first leg of the course. When the clock says there are four minutes remaining before the start, the boat leaves the immediate starting area and sails away from the line for two minutes, then tacks or jibes around and sails directly back to the previously chosen, favored spot on the line. In theory, the boat should arrive at the line as the starting gun is fired. However, there may be many variables to upset this timing. 1. Current. A strong current running at right angles to the line will speed up or slow down the final run back to the line. Several prac-

Committee boat has just started a division of Blue Jays

tice runs down and back, timed with a stop watch, will determine the current's effects. 2. The wind may not be constant. If it suddenly goes light, the run away from the line should be shortened, or if the wind picks up, the sails should be luffed to slow the boat down. 3. Another craft may get in the way. In most cases one should start on starboard tack so a right of way exists over port-tack boats. A skipper who can judge the speed of his boat will be able to make reasonable compensations for the variables. A basic plan for the start, even though it may later require amendment, is better than no plan at all.

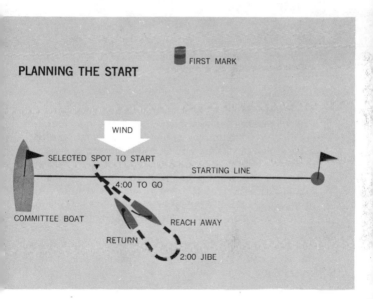

PLANNING THE START

FIRST MARK

WIND

SELECTED SPOT TO START

STARTING LINE

4:00 TO GO

COMMITTEE BOAT

REACH AWAY

RETURN

2:00 JIBE

Racing to Windward

Windward leg is always most important part of the course

■ Decisiveness—not physical prowess or great intellect —is the real key to success in racing. Every race requires ceaseless evaluation of many factors—wind, current, competition, sail trim—and an ability to resolve the best move. He who hesitates is truly lost. Not every decision need be a positive one, however, and there is a strongly held philosophy that the way to success is to do little or nothing out of the ordinary, and to wait for the opposition to blunder. Because the pitfalls along the way are so numerous, the sailing of the windward leg is the most important part of the course. The skipper who makes the fewest mistakes on this leg (usually the opening **116** one) is in a good position to win.

Pointing means sailing as high to the wind as possible

The windward leg has three elements: 1) the boat, which should be sailed as fast as it can possibly go; 2) the wind, never constant for long, which must be used to its best potential, and 3) the competition, which ideally is kept at a respectful distance. Humble threads or ribbons are keys to fast sailing. These are tied on the shrouds and are commonly called "telltales" because they tell where the wind is coming from. In time the helmsman learns at just what angle of the telltale his boat goes fastest and he steers so that the ribbon on the windward shroud will hold this angle. Of course, he must also know the right trim of his sails and the proper feel on the tiller. A feature of racing for every helmsman **117**

Skipper aboard Blue Jay #168 concentrates on the telltale

RACING TO WINDWARD

is the concentration required to make sure that the telltale angle, the sail trim, and the feel on the tiller are
always as they should be. Mistakes? A boat sailed too
close to the wind (pinching) slows down and this error
will quickly lose a race. Another is oversteering, meaning too much yawing back and forth on the tiller. This
creates rudder drag, slowing the boat. Embellishments
help. For example, when a puff strikes, the boat can be
steered higher into the wind (pointing) without losing
speed. On these legs the skipper who points his boat
the highest, without pinching, will get to the turning
118   mark first. Because the windward mark is set in the eye

of the wind, everyone must tack to it. When pondering a tack, clear air is the first consideration because all boats leave a turbulence in the air and on the water that bothers other boats. To sail in free air is desirable, so neighbors should be avoided. But to keep clear air may require tacking and this can be overdone. Every time a boat comes about it slows down, so the fewer tacks the better. Sometimes one may choose to engage a foe at close quarters, taking away his air (blanketing), or sailing so that he cannot pass (covering). The trouble with covering is that others may sail away, leaving the antagonists next-to-last and last. Another choice is to tack away from the fleet, gambling on a wind shift way over there. A gamble may bring a first, but more often a last. In fleet racing the best course to windward is usually the collective course.

Two blanketing situations. Lead boats have others' wind

Downwind

■ A big factor in downwind racing is how fast the spinnaker can be set up at the beginning of the leg and how long it can be kept aloft before dousing at the end. When this big sail is pulling, it adds so much speed that the crew which has theirs up the longest stands the best chance to pass others. Once the spinnaker is up and drawing, many sailors have a tendency to relax and wait for the next windward leg. This can be a deadly mistake. More and more skippers have come to conclude that races can easily be won or lost downwind, especially in the planing boats which accelerate and pass others so swiftly. As with the windward legs, the three elements to racing downwind are the boat, the wind, the competi-

Spinnakers take on odd shapes when full. Compare these

Right: Boat #10 has a better spinnaker set than his foe

Always keep foot of spinnaker parallel to water

Star boats have no spinnaker, but wing out the jib instead

DOWNWIND

tion. Maximum speed depends upon extracting maximum pull from the spinnaker by means of correct set and trim A fundamental is always to keep the foot of the sail absolutely parallel to the water. Also the spinnaker pole should always ride perpendicular to the mast. And it should stand at the same level as the tack, to which its outer end is secured. The pole should not tilt skyward nor droop to the water, because this will bend the spinnaker out of shape. The sail should have a belly and lift to it, accomplished by careful trimming of sheet and guy. On calm days, lightweight sheets will help the sail to lift itself. As for the jib, it should be brought down fast, so that it does not interfere when the spinnaker is broken out.

Left: #7 is blanketing #1   Right: Close quarters downwind

And it should go up before the spinnaker is dropped at the end of the leg. Ideally, the wind should come over the stern quarter of the boat for the best spinnaker angle. But the skipper must steer the shortest course to the next mark and the sail should be trimmed for this course, perhaps even jibed in case of wind shifts. The telltale (or similar wind pennant atop the mast) is just as important on this leg as on any other.

At the start of the run, the skipper should sight the next mark and check the competition. Downwind sailing presents opportunities to run up on those ahead, blanket their wind with the spinnaker, and perhaps pass them. One should try to blanket others ahead and avoid being blanketed by those behind.

Rounding

■ As with racing automobiles, horses and humans, the boat that takes a turn on the inside is better off than the opposition to the outside. There are other considerations when rounding yacht-racing marks, and a primary one is to approach the turn on the starboard tack, so as to have the right of way over the port-tack boats. In sailing the windward leg, the wise skipper always plans ahead so he will have a starboard tack at the end. A wasteful mistake that can cost a race is to overstand. This means pointing too high above the mark so that the boat has to sail back down to the turn at the end of the windward leg with sheets eased. To hit the mark right on the nose takes judgment and experience.

Boat #14 (far right) starts easy turn while #25 aims for inside

The turn itself should be done easily because a boat that is jammed around with a quick thrust of the tiller will slow and lose headway. The turn should be close to the buoy, but not too close, for any boat that strikes a mark of the course is immediately disqualified. A good rule is to steer wide of the mark on its near side, then head up smartly on the far side as the turn is completed. A boat finishing a turn close to the mark may be able to slip inside to windward of someone ahead who has sagged off. However, a turn that is begun with too wide a swing will invite a trailing boat to sneak inside, closer to the mark. If current is a factor on the course, recognize that it can help or hinder the rounding. **125**

Reaching

■ The main factor when racing on a reach is sail trim. Since all the boats are on the same direct-line course to the mark under similar wind conditions, it is difficult for one to pass another. However, the boat that has the best chance to make money is the one with perfectly trimmed sails for maximum speed at all times. This does not mean the sails are set, then ignored while the crew socializes. Rather the sail trimmers should constantly attend to their duties, playing the sheets so as to keep the sails full, on the edge of a luff. A spinnaker can be used effectively on broad reaches. In many borderline cases it may be difficult to judge on the prior leg if the boat can next carry a spinnaker. Prepare to set one anyway and save the decision until the turn has been completed and the angle of the wind on the new course can be accurately determined. On close reaches, a spinnaker usually is a liability because it will drag the boat to leeward, off the proper course. A spinnaker on a reach is set the same way—at right angles to the wind

Dinghy with best sail trim will surely reach the fastest

—which means the pole goes forward on the windward side, right up to the headstay if necessary. Keeping one's wind clear is again a must and therefore there is little profit in mixing with competitors. The boat should be set on her best lines at a slight heel. In light air, the crew sits to leeward to give the boat this heel. But in heavy weather the leeward rail must be kept clear of the water, with crew riding to windward and perhaps the mainsail luffing to spill a little unnecessary wind.

The position of the centerboard is vital on reaches and when sailing downwind. The board does not need to be down all the way, as on windward legs when it acts as a force to drive the boat ahead. Downwind, the board serves no purpose; rather it is an underwater drag and therefore should be pulled up. On a reach, a part of the board is exposed to prevent leeward drift, and the exact amount is again a matter of experience. Try it halfway down, then experiment with various positions until you achieve satisfactory speed.

Clear wind (left) is vital. #4446 (right) is blanketed

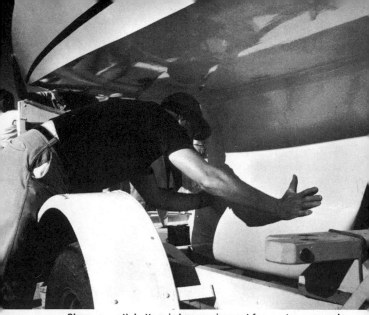

Clean, smooth bottom is key requirement for maximum speed

Tuning for Racing

■ A comment often heard among yachtsmen is, "There's nothing like a fast boat to make a skipper look good." This may be valid, but overlooks the fact that the boat had to be tuned properly to go fast and the skipper had to do his own tuning. The art of tuning concerns the proper adjustment of the interrelated elements of the boat—mast, rigging, sails—to produce maximum speed. These adjustments never cease and the wise skipper is one who constantly hovers over his boat, checking rigging, oiling fittings, climbing the mast for inspections. He's not fussing, he's tuning.

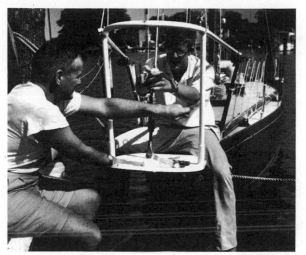
Two crewmen are taking up on turnbuckle of the headstay

Tuning begins with the mast, which must stand straight to the centerline of the boat, leaning neither to windward nor leeward. From fore and aft, looking at the boat in profile, the mast may be raked a bit one way or the other according to the skipper's preference and experience. The way to check for bends and bows is to look up the mast from deck level or a few feet away from the stern. If there is a bend it will show. The mast is supported, and can be bent, by the stays. These adjust with turnbuckles and by letting off and taking up on them, the mast will assume its proper shape.

TUNING FOR RACING

The shrouds running to the side of the boat will set the mast straight with the boat's centerline. The shrouds do not have to be taut as violin strings; in fact, some prefer them quite loose. When the boat is underway, the sails lay over to leeward, exerting a great pull on the mast and the supporting shrouds to windward. The windward shrouds then are taut as they hold the force of the sails and the mast. The leeward ones, on the other hand, have no forces pulling at them and they stand loose. The rake of the mast forward or aft is related to the feel on the tiller when sailing to windward. This is called helm. A boat with weather helm is one that wants to sail right up into the wind when the skipper takes his hand off the tiller, while one with lee helm wants to do just the opposite. Too much helm finds the tiller tugging at the skipper, who must fight its tendencies in order to stay on his course. The preference is

Instructor emphasizes crucial importance of taut jibstay

Crew in boatswain's chair checks the sail track on mast

for slight weather helm, rather than none, because this reminds the skipper to try to point his boat as high as possible and will help him to do so. To correct for too much weather helm, the top of the mast is moved forward by taking up on the headstay and letting out on the backstay. For no helm or excessive lee helm, rake the mast further aft. Another aspect of tuning is to obtain the correct fit of the sails, the most important single element in racing. The right fit depends a lot on the standing rigging. For example, the jibstay must be set up as taut as possible for the jib's benefit. A loose jibstay means the jib will sag off and the boat will point very poorly as a result.

Know the Rules

▪ The racing rules not only cover the basic right-of-way conditions (Chapter 3), but also situations encountered at the start, when overtaking, and turning marks. Copies of the complete racing rules may be obtained, at 50 cents each, by writing the North American Yacht Racing Union, 37 West 44th Street, New York 36, N.Y. Highlighted here are some of the important situations that every racing skipper should know.

Because the fleet is sailing in extremely close quarters, the start of the yacht race is a period fraught with complications and dangers. The rules say, in effect, that a yacht starts when, after the starting signal, any part of its hull or equipment first crosses the starting line in the direction of the first mark. The race committee shall endeavor to notify a yacht that has started prematurely by sounding one short blast on a sound signal for each yacht recalled, and by displaying or calling out its number or name. Failure to notify a yacht of its premature start shall not relieve it from the necessity of making a proper start. As soon as the yacht has done so, it shall be so informed by the committee (Rules 9 and 10).

While maneuvering in the starting area prior to a start, one yacht that is clearly ahead of another may alter course by bearing off in front of the trailing yacht. This may be done "but only slowly," as the rule says, so that the other will have time to change course if it so desires. The advantage to the lead boat in altering course here would be to upset the timing and get in the way of the competitor, forcing him to change his starting plans (Rule 32.3). Similarly, a leeward yacht may luff a windward one before the start. To luff another means to sail higher into the wind, so that if the luff

132

continues the boat is finally headed directly into the wind. The windward yacht is obligated to respond by also luffing in order to prevent collision with the leeward yacht. The leeward yacht alters its course to start the luff, but can do this "only slowly," to allow the other sufficient time to respond. However, the leeward yacht may luff only when it is behind the other, so that "the helmsman of the windward yacht (sighting abeam from his normal station) is aft of the mainmast of the leeward yacht" (Rule 32.3). If the leeward yacht does not have this position, it has no right to luff.

Also in a starting situation, a windward yacht cannot alter its course to sail down on top of a leeward vessel, perhaps forcing the latter to alter course (Rule 32.3). If the windward vessel does so, there are grounds for a protest by the leeward skipper and a subsequent disqualification by the race committee.

The advantage of luffing another boat is widely debated by racing enthusiasts. The theory holds that the windward boat can be made to sail so high into the wind that it will lose all headway; then the leeward yacht, which has not had to sail quite so high, can pass the other. On starting lines windward yachts can sometimes be luffed right over the line before the gun, or to the wrong side of a starting mark. But this is delicate work.

When starting, it is mandatory that skippers understand the famous anti-barging rule. Imagine the starting area in the shape of a rectangle, with the actual starting line at one short end of the box. Those who are about to start may sail within the area of this box. They cannot, within the last seconds before the starting gun, swoop into the area from beyond the windward side of the box, thereby forcing room for themselves on the line. This is barging, a descriptive name for the most common rule violation in yacht racing. Barging yachts have no rights and they cause colossal traffic jams that often result in boats colliding with one another.

At first reading, the rule covering barging is hardly crystal clear. But continued study shows that it contains all the elements necessary to curb this flagrant fouling: "But on approaching the starting line to start, a leeward yacht shall be under no obligation to give room to any windward yacht on the same tack to pass to leeward of a mark of the starting line . . ." (Rule 34.2).

However, once the starting signal has sounded, the anti-barging rule no longer applies and the leeward yacht cannot luff up so as to deprive the windward yacht of room at the mark. In practice, the skipper of the leeward boat holds his course straight toward the line and if there should be room between his craft and the mark, then the yacht to windward is entitled to fill this room (Rule 34.2). If no room exists, the windward yacht will have to get out of the way or be protested. Once the race has started and the yachts are out on the course, a situation may arise where one is overtaking the other. In explaining definitions, the rules say: "A yacht is overtaking another when she is overhauling her from clear astern, regardless of their respective courses. An overlap exists between two yachts when neither is clear astern of the other" (Rule 30).

As with the right-of-way rules, the overtaken yacht is the privileged one, the overtaking yacht the burdened one that must keep clear. Once the passing situation develops, with both on the same tack, the windward yacht must keep clear of the leeward one. This means the windward one cannot sail down to the leeward yacht and take its wind. On the other hand, should the overtaking yacht establish an overlap to leeward it must give the windward yacht "ample room and opportunity to fulfill her newly-acquired obligation to keep clear of the leeward yacht" (Rule 33.2). In other words, no harassment of the burdened vessel, please.

When it comes to two or more yachts rounding a mark of the course, the existence or non-existence of an overlap is vital. Should there be an overlap among two or more, then the yachts on the outside of the turn must give room so that those on the inside can round (Rule 34.1). But if there is no overlap, the yacht which stands clear astern must keep clear when the yacht ahead reaches the mark (Rule 34.1b). The latter is never under an obligation to give room before any overlap is firmly established. In the event of a protest, the onus lies on the inside yacht to prove that the overlap was established in proper time (Rule 34.1d). These rules stress the advantage for the yacht sailing behind on the inside to establish an overlap on the boat ahead. The leader then must give buoy room and, by the very nature of the turn, the inside yacht will go ahead of the other.

The racing rules spell out several right-of-way situations that expand the rules of the road (Rule 33). We know that a port-tack yacht must keep clear of a starboard-tack yacht. When two are on the same tack, the windward yacht must keep clear of a leeward yacht. A yacht while tacking or jibing shall keep clear of a yacht on a tack. A yacht may not tack so as to invite the probability of collision with another which, owing to her position, cannot keep out of the way. This rule prevents one yacht from causing the other to commit a foul.   135

7
It's Up to the Skipper

■ A man's sailboat is much like his home when it comes to extending hospitality. He is the host and those he invites for a sail are his guests. While on board, everyone's manners should reflect this. The skipper also should be the boss, because there is an element of danger on the water and someone must always have the authority to command action. However, this does not mean that the skipper barks orders all afternoon. He should tell his guests politely what he would like them to do, he should say please, and pass out an occasional compliment for a job well done. Guests who find themselves being shouted at may not come back, and most sailboats are hard to sail alone.

The skipper is entitled to expect certain things from his guests, too. The first thing he will look at when the day's crew comes down the pier is footgear. Soft or rubber-sole shoes are a must. Leather soles scratch paint and varnish, and spiked high heels are as out of place on a small sailboat as skirts. If invited for a sail, or to serve as crew, ask experienced sailors what to wear—and expect to get wet. Few boats are bone-dry.

While the host is usually prepared to supply some refreshments, the perfect guest will bring along an expendable present a six-pack of Cokes, a package of cheese—and a willingness to share in the work of rigging and running the boat when asked. Many novices at sailing are appalled at the compactness of the cockpit and its maze of ropes. The best mode of conduct is to sit quietly (never stand) and stay out of the way of others, especially the helmsman, until asked to move. In time the puzzles will become clear, provided the neophyte watches how the boat is rigged and sailed.

Sailing can be strenuous work for skipper and crew alike

IT'S UP TO THE SKIPPER

There is a code of etiquette for yachting, and although many of the older rituals have been abandoned in favor of modern practicality, there are still some sensible do's and dont's. It is rude, for example, to visit someone else's boat without asking permission. "May I come aboard?" addressed to the skipper, is the standard gambit. "Help thy neighbor" is a cardinal rule, as well. Boats always go without hesitation to the aid of others in distress. This is a courtesy that sometimes saves lives. Fishing boats should be given a wide berth. The keel of a sailboat can cut fishing lines and generate considerable antagonism. Refuse and garbage may be dumped overboard in the wide open spaces—provided they will sink before washing up on someone's beach. But never, never throw out trash in harbors, compact anchorages, or on small, populated lakes.

Play in port and more hard work (right) grinding a winch

The display of flags involves an etiquette all its own. No harm will come from flying the wrong flag at the wrong time in the wrong place, but such action indicates abysmal ignorance on the part of the offending skipper, if not plain bad taste. The United States ensign is the flag flown by most powerboats and many sailboats. The ensign flies during the day, between morning and evening colors. Sloop-rigged sailboats carry it on a staff at the stern when at anchor. When underway it is flown at the leech of the mainsail, sewn to the sail about two-thirds of the length of the leech above the clew. The triangular yacht club burgee flies at the top of the mast (called the truck) when underway or at anchor. The owner's private signal, a rarity among the small sailboat fraternity, may be flown at the truck in place of the burgee, although the latter is preferred.

139

Anchor, paddle, bucket, life jackets, line are essential

Extra Gear

■ Stowage space is always invaluable aboard a sailboat because many items of extra gear must be carried. Some are extra in the sense that the boat can do without them —for instance, a mop for swabbing decks. Some—such as a pump—are essential. Stow gear efficiently and always in the same place, so it is readily available.

ESSENTIAL

Pump: Lightweight plastic ones are ideal, provided they have an extension which will carry water overboard.

140 **Tools:** Pliers and screwdriver will have many uses.

Compass (left) costs under $5. Air horn is about $12

Anchor: See Chapter III for recommended types, sizes.
Lights: A search or flash type is a must on all boats.
Life Jackets: Have enough to equal the seating capacity of the boat. Buoyant cushions may be substituted.
Paddle: Necessary when wind dies or boat is grounded.
Compass: Have one working in case fog rolls in.
Bucket and Sponge: They will have dozens of uses when it comes to keeping deck, cockpit, and bilges clean.
Whistle or Horn: To signal others when sailing at night.
Painter: For tying up the boat. Spinnaker sheets may be substituted at a dock or when being towed.

EXTRA GEAR

Spare Parts: Cotter pins, extra shackles, snap hooks, twine, tape, and sail stops, all belong below decks.
Resusitube: This plastic tube, costing $1.50, is recommended for administering artificial respiration.

NON-ESSENTIAL

Outboard: Many sailboats have brackets which hold outboard motors. They come in handy when the wind dies. Lightweight motors with extra-length shafts are best. The British Sea Gull weighs 28 pounds, costs $140.
Foul-Weather Gear: Carry several suits for the crew.
Portable Radio: It can provide weather information.
Binoculars: They are helpful at spotting course marks.
Fenders: Use them to protect topsides when docking.

Thermos jug

Searchlight

Outboard motor

Buoyant cushion

Foul-weather gear

Clove hitch to a cleat (above) secures sheets and halyards

Figure-8's at ends stop lines from running through blocks

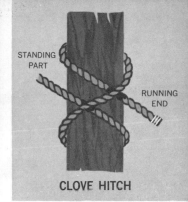

STANDING PART

RUNNING END

CLOVE HITCH

Loop is pulled tight to the cleat

Marlinespike Seamanship

■ Since sailboats are controlled by ropes (lines, sheets, halyards), every sailor must be able to tie a few basic knots quickly and accurately. One of the easiest is a clove hitch to a cleat, shown in the three pictures above. The line is given a turn and a half around the cleat, then a loop is dropped over one projecting end of the cleat and pulled tight. The only objection to this clove hitch comes when great strains are set up on a sheet and the hitch is pulled so tight that it becomes difficult to free in a hurry. The alternative is merely to wrap the sheet around the cleat three times. The clove hitch is a quick and reliable means to secure a line to a spar or to a piling on a pier (above). The way to tie it is to make a loop in the line and drop the loop over the spar. Then make a second loop, with the running end on the underside of the loop, drop that over the spar and pull the line tight. The running end (or bight) is that section of the line used in the knot and beyond, while the standing part secures the boat to the pier. **145**

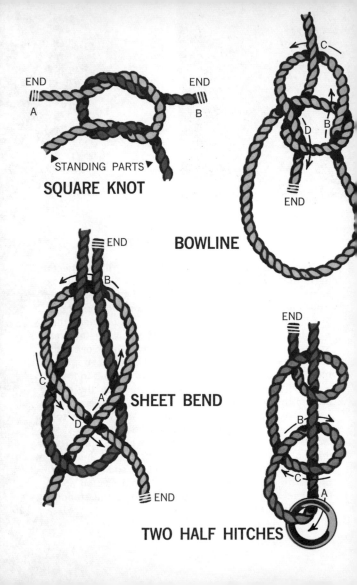

SQUARE KNOT

BOWLINE

SHEET BEND

TWO HALF HITCHES

The reef or square knot is used in reefing and for joining two pieces of rope. The knot is tied (see illustration at left) by passing A over and under B. Then form a loop with A. Pass B around the back of the loop and then through it. Pull the ends tight. Make sure the end of the line and the standing part come out of the loop on the same side. If they are on opposite sides, it is a "granny knot" which may slip or jam.

The bowline is a knot that will neither slip nor jam. It can be used as a sling, a safety belt, or when an eye is needed in the end of the rope. Make a loop (A) in the standing part of the line. Pass the end (B) up through the loop, around the back of the standing part (C), then return it down through the loop and draw it tight.

The sheet bend is generally used to join ropes of unequal sizes. Make a loop in the end of the larger line (grey). Pass the end of the smaller rope (white) through the loop (A), around in back (B), then in front (C), and under its own standing part (D).

The easiest way to secure the end of a line to another object, such as a spar or a mooring eye, is with the half hitch. Two half hitches will make the knot stronger. Pass the rope through the eye or ring (A). Then it goes under and around the standing part (B and C). Repeat the turns to make two half hitches.

There are several more knots in the nautical lexicon, but these will suffice for the beginner. Generally, a bend is a knot that unites two rope ends, while a hitch secures a rope to another object. For greater strength and permanence, splicing rather than knotting is used to join two ropes, or for making a loop or eye on the end of a rope. Splicing is a more difficult art and one worthy of a real, live instructor.

147

Maintenance

■ All boats require some maintenance on the part of their owners. This is true even of the fiberglass hulls, despite those advocates who claim no upkeep. Not so, although fiberglass boats may require smaller expenditures of time and money because they do not require painting once or more each season.

The way to make boat maintenance a mere chore, rather than sheer toil, is to keep at it, spreading the work over the entire year. Such preventive maintenance will avoid, for a long time, the back-breaking jobs, such as scraping the paint off the hull down to the bare wood or recanvassing the deck. Daily maintenance, in season, means cleanliness: keeping bilges dry, decks swabbed,

A trim boat means care and attention the year around, but doing a little at a time reduces labor. Many boat yards permit owners to do their own repairs.

cockpits tidy. Also checking the running rigging and replacing lines when they show signs of wear. At midseason the skipper should conduct a complete check of his boat: running rigging, standing rigging, sails, fittings, the hull, and promptly make whatever repairs or replacements appear to be necessary.

Maintenance means a check list, a master sheet containing all the elements of the sailboat subject to wear and tear. And the check list should be followed by a things-to-do list.

There are five general areas of maintenance, beginning with the hull. Nicks, scrapes and gouges should be smoothed with sandpaper, then carefully filled with **149** a plastic wood compound or filler. For fiberglass hulls, special kits of glass roving and resin for patching are available at most marine stores. Secondly, there is the matter of loose fittings—fairleads and chocks for example, or seats and rails if they have split or worked free. Check them and tighten where necessary.

Third, there is the leaking boat, a disappearing phenomenon, thanks to modern glues and crack sealers for wood. (Fiberglass hulls seldom leak.) If the bilge is continually filling while the boat is at a mooring, the drastic solution is to haul it out of water, locate the leak and fill with a waterproof sealer. Fourth, we come to painting and varnishing. Use marine paints and varnishes exclusively, as other kinds are useless. Never paint or varnish over old surfaces without first sanding thoroughly for absolute smoothness. In salt water, and even fresh water where fouling and marine growths are prevalent, use special anti-fouling paints for the bottom of the boat. Fiberglass boats, after a few seasons of use will look a lot better if they are painted with Epoxy-resin paints, extremely durable and hard.

The fifth category concerns out-of-season storage. Many sailboats adapt to a trailer and can be stored at home. If the trailer is a good one, it will give plenty of support for the hull. The alternative is to take the boat to a yard and store it in a cradle. Many yards permit the owner to do much of his own work, such as putting the cover on or cleaning the bilge. The cover should permit air to circulate freely below so that rot will not start. And the bilge should be drained dry. Year-around maintenance is worthwhile on two scores. A handsome boat reflects pride of ownership and a well-kept one will command a better sale price.

Hulls should be sanded smooth before applying new paint

Cranes pick boats from the water and set them In cradles

Buying a Boat

■ Buying a boat is an exciting adventure, one fraught with dangers and hedged with advice. The old salts like to tell beginners that they should first know what they want to use the boat for and how much they want to pay. Then the novice is supposed to find the kind of craft that fills his two requirements but, alas, this is almost impossible. The beginner is not equipped to analyze what he expects from a boat, nor can he equate costs with desires. So no wonder the surveys show the owner's first sailboat is only kept for one or two seasons before being traded for another. By that time the novice is an old salt himself, he knows what his next boat will be. When starting from scratch, the beginner's best bet is to look around at the common types that have found wide acceptance with the local sailors. Copying is no sin, provided the most popular craft in the harbor is not a tricky planing boat that a novice could not begin to handle. There are other fundamentals, too. Depth of water, for instance: Don't buy a keel boat to sail in shoal waters. Weather must be considered. An over-canvassed craft would be a liability where the prevailing winds seldom dip below 20 knots, while small sail areas will not push much weight through doldrums. Consider the cat boat's simple single-sail rig, but lean toward a sloop instead. The cat can be sailed alone and is nice for practice. But its unbalanced rig does not have the performance or the feel of the sloop, to which most sailors soon graduate. A keel boat cannot capsize, but it costs more to buy and to keep, while the center-boarder has more room, has more feel, and will react faster for the beginner. Fiberglass is preferable to wood, at least in the eyes of the manufacturers, who are

Used boats can be good buys but deserve close inspection

building more and more sailboats of this material.

The ideal first sailboat? There is no accounting for taste, but it should almost certainly have a big, comfortable cockpit to sit in, not one where the crew has to hang out over the rail to keep the right side up. The hull might very well be an ample-beamed, centerboarder with either a fiberglass, rounded hull, such as a 16-foot Day Sailer, or a plywood hard-chine hull, such as a 13-foot Blue Jay. Where does one buy these boats? Hopefully from the local marine dealer, although he may not have the perfect one. Fortunately, more and more dealers are taking on sailboats and so the selection of models widens. Boat shows provide excellent opportunities for looking over the fleet, but there is little one can do to learn about a craft's performance in the bone-dry exhibition hall. The boat show's favorite gesture, rapping the hulls with the knuckles for resonance, **153** proves nothing. So a show is a place for looking—but buy later after a local demonstration on home waters.

What about a second-hand boat? Certainly this is a money-saving way, but buyer beware! Although the initial price may be attractive, the expense of putting the used boat into proper trim can bankrupt a budget. With wooden boats, look out if they have been on dry land for a long time. The seams may have opened, which can mean recalking—a tedious do-it-yourself project or a costly one at the yard. If the paint has peeled, suspect dry rot in the planking. Take a penknife and poke around. If the knife slips into the wood as though it were butter, pass the boat up. In the south, look carefully for the tiny pin holes in the paint that may well mean toredos, the marine boring worm. With fiberglass boats, look on the inside of the hull under the decks for repair patches, and inspect them to make sure a good job was done. In plywood craft, check the corners where two sheets join and also the fastenings. The open edges exposing the laminations can absorb water which promotes rot, while common nail fastenings will show rust. Broken ribs or frames must be replaced; an expensive business. If there is any reason to question the condition of the boat, professional advice should be sought by the prospective purchaser. A surveyor, for a small fee, will inspect the vessel and deliver a report. Where thousands of dollars are involved, a survey is mandatory. Prices for used sailboats will wander all over the lot. However, many boats, particularly the more recent fiberglass ones, depreciate slowly at a rate of 10 to 15 per cent per year, which is a lot lower than comparable outboard runabouts. The person who would know prices best is the yacht broker. This specialist is like a real-estate broker and operates on commissions. If there are problems, take them to the broker for honest advice. This fellow can also arrange for the charter of sailboats, usually of the cruising kind, 25 feet and over. A charter, for a week or a month, is a good way to get to know a boat before making a purchase. The cost is on a flat-fee basis.

As for new-boat prices, most of the logical, first-purchase sailboats in the 14- to 20-foot sizes cost from $1,000 to $2,000. Below $1,000 come most of the dinghies, in fiberglass or wood. You-build-it kits are available for several models, and they cut costs from 25 to 50 per cent, although most have poor resale value.

Sailboat displays at the boat shows are growing larger

The Language of Sailing

ABAFT: Toward the stern. The tiller is abaft the mast.

ABEAM: At right angles to the fore-and-aft centerline of the boat. Off the beam or on the side of the boat.

BACKSTAYS: Rope or wire cable leading aft from the mast for the purpose of supporting this spar.

BALLAST: Heavy material, lead or iron, placed in the bottom of some boats to give stability.

BEAM: The maximum width measurement of a vessel.

BEARING: The direction of one object from another.

BEAT: To sail to windward.

BEND: To secure or to make fast a sail to a spar. Also the knot by which one rope is made fast to another.

BILGE: Bottom part of the hull adjacent to the keel.

BROACH: A vessel running downwind swings broadside to the wind. Dangerous in high seas.

CHAIN PLATES: Metal plates bolted to the side of the boat to which the stays are attached.

CHOCK: A metal casting, usually at the bow, through which the mooring line is led.

CLEAT: A wood or metal fitting with horns to which lines are secured. Cam or jam cleats provide quick release.

CLEW: The lower, aft corner of a sail.

CLOSE HAULED: Sailing as close to the wind as possible with sails trimmed flat.

COAMING: Raised framework or railing around the cockpit to keep out water.

COCKPIT: Open area behind the mast where crew and skipper sit. Some are self-draining.

CRINGLE: A metal or rope eye sewn into the sail at clew, tack or head, to which sheet or halyard is attached by means of a shackle.

CUDDY: A decked shelter, smaller than the cabin, for protection of the crew aft of the mast.

DAGGERBOARD: A metal or wooden board extending through a boat's bottom, similar to a centerboard.

DOWNHAUL: Block and tackle which pulls down the mainsail to improve its shape when hoisted.

DRAFT: The depth of water a boat requires to float free of the bottom.

EASE: To let out on the sheet so as to relieve the pressure on the sail and perhaps spill some wind.

EBB: Ebb tide is falling from high to low. Ebb current is flowing out to sea. Opposite is flood.

FAIRLEAD: An eyelet fitting which changes the direction of a sheet or halyard led through it.

FETCH: A boat sailing to windward can fetch its objective without having to make an additional tack.

FID: A wood marlinespike, or a block at the heel of the mast holding it in place.

FOOT: Lower edge of a sail.

FRAMES: The ribs of the hull to which planking is attached. Ribs terminate at the keel.

FREE: Sailing with the wind aft.

FREEBOARD: That part of the vessel above the water.

FURL: To roll a sail snugly on boom or yard.

GAFF: A spar used to support the head of the mainsail, hence gaff-rigged, an older type of rigging.

GARBOARD: (Or strake). Hull planks nearest the keel.

GENOA: A large, overlapping jib first introduced in an international 6-meter race at Genoa, Italy.

GOOSENECK: A metal fitting, usually a universal joint,

securing the boom to the mast.

GUDGEON: An eye fitting into which the rudder's pintles are inserted. Located on the transom of small sailboats.

GUNWALE: The rail of the boat at deck level.

HALYARD: Rope or wire used to hoist sails.

HARD-A-LEE: Final command sounded as a boat begins to come about. First command is "Ready about."

HATCH: An opening in the deck, with a cover, for access to the cabin below.

HEAD: The top corner of a sail. Also a toilet.

HEADSTAY: The forward stay supporting the mast. Also called jibstay or forestay. Some boats have both.

HEAD-TO-WIND: Bow headed into the wind, sails luffing.

HEADWAY: Forward motion of the boat.

HEEL: The tilt or tipping action caused by wind.

HELM: The rudder or tiller steering the boat.

HIKE: To climb or lean out to windward, counteracting excessive heeling of the hull.

IRONS: When tacking, a boat that will not come about but lays head-to-wind is said to be in irons.

JIBE: To change tacks by turning away from the wind.

JIBSTAY: Forward stay on which the jib is hoisted.

JIGGER: The shorter mast aft on a yawl or ketch.

KEDGE: A small anchor.

KEEL: The lowest part of the hull, the backbone of the ship, running its entire length.

LEEWARD: Away from the direction of the wind.

LEECH: The after edge of a sail.

LUFF: Forward edge of a sail. Also to sail the boat closer to the wind so air will spill from the sails.

MARLINESPIKE: A pointed wooden or metal instrument used to open up strands of rope or wire.

158   MIZZEN: The shorter mast aft on a yawl or ketch.

MOORING: The chain or rope, buoy and anchor to which a boat is secured when not sailing.

OFF THE WIND: Sailing any course except one to windward, which is called "on the wind."

OUTHAUL: Line and fitting used to secure clew of a sail.

OVERSTAND: To sail beyond an object, such as a buoy.

PAINTER: Short line used to secure the bow to a landing.

PINCH: To sail a boat too close to the wind.

POINTING: Sailing close to the wind.

PRAM: Rectangular dinghy with square bow.

QUARTER: Side of boat aft of the beam, forward of stern.

REEVE: To pass lines through block or fairlead.

ROACH: Outward curve of the leech of a sail.

RUNNING: Sailing before the wind.

SHACKLE: A U-shaped metal fitting with a pin or screw across the open end, used to join sheets to sails.

SHEAVE: The wheel inside a block.

SHEET: Line used to trim sails.

SHROUDS: Wires or ropes supporting the mast.

SPAR: Term for masts, booms, spinnaker poles, etc.

SPREADER: Horizontal strut on the mast for its support.

TACK: Lower, forward corner of a triangular sail. Also a boat tacks when it changes its direction and the angle at which the wind strikes its sails.

TENDER: A sailboat lacking stability, opposite of stiff.

TILLER: A wooden bar fitting to the rudder, for steering.

TRANSOM: The stern facing of the hull.

TRAVELER: Metal rod at stern for trimming mainsail.

TRIM: To set the sails at the correct angle to the wind.

VANG: A line to steady the boom when off the wind.

WHISKER-POLE: A light pole or stick extending from the mast and used to hold the jib out when off the wind.

WINDWARD: Toward the wind, opposed to leeward. **159**